T0193648

Tickle Your Funny Bone

FUNNY TALES FROM EVERYDAY LIFE

Dr. J. Terry Hall and Ben F. Hall

authorHOUSE®

AuthorHouse™
1663 Liberty Drive
Bloomington, IN 47403
www.authorhouse.com
Phone: 1 (800) 839-8640

Published by AuthorHouse 10/03/2018

ISBN: 978-1-5462-5998-5 (sc)
ISBN: 978-1-5462-5997-8 (e)

Library of Congress Control Number: 2018910989

Print information available on the last page.

Author's Notes

There are many people who provided support and encouragement in the process of compiling this book. A big "thank you" goes to all who contributed their personal experiences. To my wonderful wife, Patricia who spent many nights alone as I worked for hours in producing this work. Thank you for hanging in there with me. A special thanks goes to our son, Ben F. Hall for all the wonderful tales involving not only his experiences, but those of our grandchildren, and I want to thank our sixteen year old grandson, Anthony Hall, for contributing many of his personal tales.

Also, a disclaimer is noted. If there are errors found in this book, they are unintentional, and are the oversight of the author. In no way do they reflect on the contributors.

Author's notes

Introduction

After working in the field of education for forty years, I wrote this book with the help of my friends in the field of education. They shared their funny tales from days gone by, to be passed on to future generations. It makes my heart warm to think their wonderful tales will be told over and over for years after they have moved on to the spiritual realm.

In this book, I have expanded my contributors to not only educators, but to anyone in any profession who would like to share experiences. There is a saying that an "apple a day keeps the doctor away," and I believe with all my being that a good belly laugh a day will do the same.

Chapter 1

Growing up on a south central Kentucky cattle farm, I always related to farm life. In addition to growing tobacco, we were proud of our registered Black Angus cattle. I always considered myself a farm boy and was proud of my heritage. The problem was I only worked in the tobacco field after the seeds had been planted in the tobacco bed, grew up to small plants, and were taken to the tobacco field for transplanting. Following planting came the hoeing, cutting, hanging it in the barn, stripping and hauling the crop to the tobacco sale barn in another town. As I said previously, I knew nothing about planting the tobacco seeds in the tobacco bed.

In my Freshman year in high school, I joined the "Future Farmers of America" and took an agriculture class. One of the first tests I had to take was a multiple choice test. One of the questions was, "How many

tobacco seeds do you need to plant a one hundred foot tobacco bed."
The choices were: A a pound, B a tea spoon or C one hundred pounds.
Using my fourteen-year-old logic, I settled on one hundred pounds. Of
course, my answer was incorrect only one teaspoon for a one hundred
foot tobacco bed was required.

For a shy fourteen year old boy, this was devastating. Needless to
say I always remembered how to plant a tobacco bed.

Dr. J. Terry Hall

Several years later I graduated from college and taught a few years in
Kentucky and Tennessee before moving to Asheville, North Carolina.
My students in Asheville were mostly city children and had never been
on a farm, much less, knew about farm life. This was before the state-
mandated curriculum and I decided it would be worthwhile to teach a
unit on animal husbandry.

As part of the unit, I was explaining the names of the farm animals.
When I asked if anyone in class had ever seen a bull, one ten-year-old
boy raised his hand and explained that he had rode a bull one time. I
was shocked and asked where this had happened. He explained that it
was at his uncle's farm. Still shocked, I asked him to show the picture

on my flash cards of the one which looked like the one he rode. He quickly picked out the animal. It was a mule!

Dr. J. Terry Hall

In 1973 my wife Patricia and I took a trip to "Animal Kingdom" in northern Virginia. We had heard how wonderful it was to see all the wild animals in their natural habitat. Arriving at the front gate, we were surprised to find that we could just drive our car through the park after paying at the gate I thought that was great, but Patricia was not too keen about the idea of being so close to the wild animals. Being the macho man that I was at the time, I assured her there was no danger as long as we stayed in the car.

It was as wonderful as I imagined. We drove by a pride of lions, sunning themselves on the side of the road. We were no more that ten feet from the lions. Patricia was afraid and kept telling me to go on down the road. Animals were everywhere! They walked around our car and many times we had to wait until the elephants crossed the road in front of us. Everything went great until we saw a group of rhino on the side of the road. I was surprised at the size of these animals. I had seen them on TV, but never live and this close. I stopped the car and started taking pictures. All of a sudden, I felt our car move. Looking back I saw our problem; a very large rhino had put his tusk under our back bumper and lifted the back of our car off the ground. All that "macho" I had felt went out the window. I hit the gas pedal only to discover the rear wheels were off the ground and we were not going anywhere! Our exhaust blew hot air in the face of the rhino, causing him to throw his head up and lift our car ever higher. By this time, Patricia and I were about to lose it! The fumes from our exhaust caused the rhino to release our car and I took off in a cloud of dust! We did not stop until we exited the gate. A few years later, we once again visited the park to find that they had installed a tram which passed several feet above the animals. It was safer, but not nearly as exciting!

Dr. J. Terry Hall

A woman came forward at church and asked for forgiveness. She said, she was guilty of vanity. Each morning as soon as she woke, she would go to her mirror and admire her beauty.

She said she would run her fingers through her long hair and admire how young her face looked, even though she was getting on up in years. The preacher said he was pleased she was seeking forgiveness, but she had the sin wrong. It was not vanity; it was imagination!

Charles Freeman

I was watching a "little league" soccer game one day and observed a young mother, yelling for her daughter. She was shouting encouragement at the top of her voice. About that time, another girl tripped her daughter as she made a play. The mother became unglued! She started shouting that the referee was blind if he could not see the foul! As she continued yelling and jumping up and down, a senior gentleman, sitting next to me, asked in a quiet voice, "Do you know the difference between a soccer mom and a pit bull dog? "I said, "No, what? "He relied, "Lipstick!"

John Moore

A rock band was playing in Owensboro, Kentucky back around the turn of the century. Rock bands can get rather wild as the night goes on. One of the rockers printed a sign to hang around his neck which said, "Girls, show me your stuff! "He turned the sign backwards and planned to flip it over at the right time. Unknown to him, other members of the band took the sign and secretly printed under his message, "I am Gay. "At the chosen time, he flipped the sign and was ready for the girls to all scream and show their stuff. He was surprised to only see shock on the faces of the audience! Looking down at the sign, he turned to his band and said between his teeth, "I will get you back!"

Paul and Cameron Lowe

I started my career in a small funeral home in west Texas. I soon took over as Manager and one of my first objectives was to run an advertisement for our services. My other Manager and I decided to play recorded music at the beginning and at the end of the advertisement. I made the decision to play a song I had heard on the radio. It was a pretty tune and almost made me cry.

After it first played, my partner called me, all excited. "Do you know the name of the tune they just played at the beginning and ending of our advertisement? "Beaming, I said, "No, but what did you think about it? "He told me the title was "Killing Me Safely! "For a long time, everyone in our small town would ask us if we were still "killing our clients safely."

Kenneth Cone

During my 53 years as an educator in five different states in the United States, I traveled to many national, state and local conferences to present or lead workshops. Several years ago, while working as a professor for a university in Kentucky, I was traveling by car and grew very tired. It was an extremely long day and I had traveled far. About 7:00 p.m., I stopped at a motel to rest for the night. I was so exhausted that I put on my bed clothes and walked over to the sink to wash my face and brush my teeth. In order to save time, I did not turn on the light. I just wanted to "get done" what needed to be done so I could go to bed. Well, I was successful in washing my face; however, when I started brushing my teeth, the toothpaste tasted horrible. I spit it out and decided to turn on the light. When I looked at the container of toothpaste, it was not toothpaste, but Hydrocortisone Cream. Immediately, I called the Poison Control Center in the city where I was spending the night. I was told to wash my mouth out good and rinse with Listerine or Scope. The gentleman on the phone was kind enough to say, "We get these calls all the time from old people." The only problem with that statement was, I was not old.

Dr. Judy Pierce

My friend Charles and I went golfing at one of the mountain courses near Asheville, North Carolina. The third hole was a 150-yard-shot from the top of the mountain. A golf path ran down the mountain with several twists and turns toward the third hole. Charles teed off first and landed on the edge of the green. Satisfied with his shot, he smiled and said, "Let's see you beat that! "I stepped up to the tee and topped my ball. The ball went maybe twenty feet and landed on the golf path where it took a big bounce, and, hit the golf path, about thirty feet from the green. Once again, jumping, it landed on the green and rolled to five inches from the hole. Charles looked at me and said, "You are not going to count that are you? "I looked up in disbelief and said, "You better believe it! That will most likely be my best shot of the game!"

Dr. J. Terry Hall

I once heard a story about an old woman who was getting on up in years and her family had decided to place her in a local nursing home. The nursing home required each patient to be evaluated to see if they qualified to be admitted. A nurse asked her if she could give herself a bath. The older woman looked shocked and said, "I take three every week. On Monday, I wash down as far as possible, on Wednesday, I wash up as far as possible and on Friday I wash possible."

Dr. J. Terry Hall

It seems this gospel preacher went up in rural Indiana to hold a Gospel Meeting. It was to be a week long meeting, beginning on a Monday night. During the first lesson, he noticed an elderly gentleman and his wife sat about three rows back. He also noticed that during his lesson the old fellow kept nodding off to sleep. However, his wife would elbow him to keep him awake. This happened almost every night of the meeting. On Friday night, just as the service began, a thunderstorm came through the area. It began to rain hard with lightening and thundering! Well, the preacher gets up and begins to preach, and about halfway through the sermon, the electricity goes out and, with it being in the country, and no other lights around, everyone was left in total darkness! The preacher tells everyone to just remain where they are and pray silently. If the lights did not come on shortly, he would dismiss the service. In the meantime, the old man had fallen asleep and during the blackout he woke up. Everyone was completely silent, until the silence was broken by the old man saying, "Damn, they have turned off all the lights! They have all left me here and gone home!

Art Harris

The following is an excerpt from a letter sent from the State Prison in Phoenix, Arizona in 1987. It was sent to a prison outreach program at the Camelback Church of Christ.

To Whom It May Concern:

My cellmate and I are heavy cigarette smokers. There was a time that we ran out of cigarette papers to roll our cigarettes. We had access to tobacco but could never find cigarette papers and we were at our "wits end."

The local Church of Christ came to the prison as part of their Missionary work and gave each prisoner a Bible. We felt we had no need for a Bible, but cigarette papers were a different thing altogether! My cellmate came up with an idea. Since the pages in the Bible were extra thin, I thought why not tear out the pages and use them to roll our cigarettes."

As we rolled our cigarettes I said, "It just don't feel right to use the Bible like this. The least we could do is to read what it said on the page before using it as rolling paper. We agreed that we would take time about reading the page torn out before rolling our cigarette." Finally, during the course of a year we read and rolled our way through the Bible. By the end of the year we were convinced that we needed to be baptized for the remission of our sins. I will be out of here in two more years, and one of the first places I plan to go is the Camelback Church of Christ to thank them for the cigarette paper. It has changed my life.

Nan Slaughter

Chapter 2

Several years ago, my aunt and her daughter were waiting for a flight out of the local airport to Texas to visit her sister. My aunt was around thirty years old and her daughter was three. As they waited, a middle aged man came over and commented on how pretty her daughter, Becky looked in her pretty dress. He said to the little girl, "Do you want to go to Texas with me? "Little Becky looked up at the stranger and said, "No, but my mama will go." My aunt's face turned red as a beet, then she quickly said, "we better let the man go alone."

Dr. J. Terry Hall

Another time my aunt was going down a rural road, and, as she rounded a curve, there was a mattress lying in the road. She couldn't miss it so she straddled the mattress. Thankful that she had not been in an accident, she continued on down the road. She heard this sound coming from her car and thought there must be something wrong with the motor. She saw a service station coming up and turned in; the attendant came up and she explained the terrible sound. He got down on his hands and knees and looked under the car. He stood up and asked, "How did you get a mattress under your car? "The mattress had caught up under the car and she had been pulling it down the road.

Dr. J. Terry Hall

Old Zek, the town drunk, decided to go to church one Sunday. When he arrived, the preacher was fired up and preaching about tithing. After the service and everybody was leaving, shaking the preacher's hand and telling him how much they appreciated the sermon, Old Zek was the next in line. The preacher reached out for old Zek's hand and said, "Well Zek, don't you think it is about time you begin tithing for the Lord? "Old Zek thought for a moment and said, "Well, preacher you know I spend ninety percent of all I make on wine, women and song. I guess I do waste the other ten percent."

Phillip Cochran

As Old Zek was known to be the town drunk, and everyone had tried to help him, but to no avail. Well, it just so happened that one Saturday afternoon, old Zek was coming down the street "about three-sheets-in-the wind. "The country store owner and the preacher saw him coming. The store owner said to the preacher, "I think I know how to stop old Zek from drinking." The preacher said, "I've got to see this." Then he said to the store owner, "What do you have in mind?" The store owner said, "I've a setting hen in the back store room and a litter of day old pups that my old hound dog just delivered. Come with me and I will show you. They both went into the back room and the store owner got a couple of the newborn puppies, whose eyes had not opened yet, and slipped them under the setting hen. Just about that time Old Zek came into the store. The preacher said, "We got something in the back we want to show you. We think that once you see this, you will stop drinking." "Well", Zek said, "I know I need to stop, so let's go see it." They all go into the store room and the owner reaches down and lifts up one side of the setting hen. Zek sees the puppies, whose eyes hadn't opened yet and says, "Well, can you believe that?" Then he said, "I will tell you what preacher, I ain't going to eat no more eggs!"

Phillip Cochran

After WWII, my mother, brother and I were living in Hobbs, New Mexico with my grandparents; waiting for my father to return. During the war, he moved through Italy to fight in the Battle of the Bulge. After the war, he was mustered out, but re-enlisted as active reserves. He was sent to Sendai Japan Tohoku Region, northeast of Tokyo on Honshu Island. Sendai is known today for the great 2011 Sendri Tsunami. A little later, we were asked to join my father in Sendai Japan. So my mother had to take two young boys across country to fly from San Francisco to Honolulu to Tokyo.

While in California, we had to stop at the Presidio Military Base to receive our shots, of which there were many. We were escorted to where a medic was going to administer the shots. When my brother realized what was going on, he bolted out the door. We couldn't find him. Soldiers were called to look for him, but he was nowhere to be found. After about two hours he was located under one of the buildings. He refused to come out. One of the soldiers had to crawl under the building and drag him out. Fighting the entire way, he had to be held down to administer the shots. Thinking, what else could go, we were transported to the San Francisco Airport.

We boarded a Pan American World Airways Clipper, departing for Honolulu with twenty-four passengers, most of them army dependents heading to Japan. After take-off, the Clipper caught fire and had to return. Of course, if it can go wrong, it will! The landing gear wouldn't come down. Still on fire and no landing gear, the pilot told everyone "as soon as the plane stopped and the door is opened, get out. "That sounded like a plan. It seemed like it took forever for the plane to come to a stop and the door opened. As soon as the door opened, my brother took off like a bullet, leaving me and my mother behind. You have to admire his sense of self-preservation! Once again, there was an all-out-search for him. They had another air plane ready to take us on to Tokyo but first we had to find my brother. About this time, I said, "Why don't we just leave him?" But mothers being mothers, mind just wouldn't hear of it. Pan American had another Douglas DC4 ready to go as soon as they got the other plane off the runway and we made it to Tokyo.

Don Carter

The Church of Christ believes the Bible teaches one is saved by being immersed in water through baptism. At the time one is baptized, Jesus adds that person to the Church if he/she believes, repents, and confesses their belief in Jesus being the Son of God.

Children have a tenancy to take everything in a literal sense. When I was a small girl, we always attended the church every time the church doors were open. When a person would come forward to be baptized, he/she would go into a room and put on white pants and shirt. The preacher, who was going to conduct the baptizing, would also put on white clothes before walking down into the baptistery to meet the new convert. She was convinced that God was personally doing the baptizing!

Patricia Hall

Another time my Uncle Bill was driving up the crooked mountain road toward Hendersonville, North Carolina. His wife and I were riding in the car. I watched as Uncle Bill cut the curves short and crossed the center line. I looked at Uncle Bill with anger on my face and shouted, "Uncle Bill, if God had meant for you to drive on the other side of the road, He would not have put that yellow line in the middle of the road."

Many many years have passed and I have a better understanding of God as revealed in the Bible, but my faith has continued to grow and will continue to grow until the Lord calls me home.

Patricia Hall

Chapter 3

Growing up in the small town of Tompkinsville, Kentucky, which had a population of around 2000 people, and where everyone not only knew everyone, but knew all their kin and just about everything about their lives.

One day, I asked my daddy, "Daddy, how many people lived in Tompkinsville when you were a boy "He was born in 1915. He said, "around 2000." I said, How do you explain it being 2000 when you were a boy and 2000 now?" He thought for a moment and said, "Well son, it seemed that every time a baby was born some man left town."

Frank Hall

When our son Ben was around two years old, and into everything, Patricia and I took him to visit some friends. Night was coming on as we sat in the living room, talking, while Ben was running around everywhere, discovering this and that. About that time he ran down a hallway and out-of-sight of the adults. My friend turned to me and commented, "That Ben is a brave little fellow. "I puffed out my chest, and, like a proud poppa said, "You got that right, he ain't afraid of nothing. "About that time, we heard this horrifying scream as Ben came running up the hallway, yelling, "The dark is going to get me! The dark is going to get me! "So much for all my bragging.

Dr. J. Terry Hall

One Saturday night old Zek was coming home really late. He was drunk as usual. He said," Yep, that's my house and that's my new car in the driveway. "He fumbled in his pocket and got his keys. He unlocked the door, and went inside. He then said, "Yep, this is my house all right and that's my wife on the sofa kissing me."

Phillip Cochran

One day the preacher and his wife went to visit a newly-married couple to invite them to church. When they knocked on the door, the young bride answered and they noticed she had been crying. The preacher's wife said, "Now dear, what's wrong and why are you crying?" The young bride said, "Well, John has gone snipe-hunting with some of the older men and, if he catches any snipes and brings them home, I don't know how to cook them."

Phillip Cochran

My grandson, Anthony is one of the joys of my life along with all of our other grandchildren. He told me this true story. He is fifteen years old and very mature for his age. He is a young Christian and seems very dedicated to the church. Being fifteen, he does not have his driver's license and I pick him up every Sunday morning to take him to church. The story he told me went something like this:

"I woke up at the regular time to get ready for church. I got dressed, combed my hair and brushed my teeth. When I opened the door, I saw that it was raining, so I took a jacket to hold over my head. Pap-paw always picks me up around 9:15 a.m. and I was right on time. I did not have a cell phone so I could not call him to see if he was coming. As the rain got harder, and the time kept creeping forward, I didn't know what to do. Since I did not have a phone, I just decided to tough it out and wait on him. At 10:15 and soaking wet, I went back into the house. I told my dad what had happened and that I finally gave up and came on inside. Dad looked at me in disbelief and said, "Son, this is Saturday!"

Anthony Hall

I was teaching "Head Start" one year and one of the little boys was absent. I asked him the next day if he had been sick the day before. He looked up and said, "Yes, I had a bad ear confection."

Elaine Burgess

Once a young girl was absent in my second grade class. Her mom sent a note the next day saying, "Jenny was absent due to pleurisy in her arm."

Elaine Burgess

During this day and time, there is a debate going on over corporeal punishment, not only in the schools but also with your own children. I am not stating my opinion on this issue at this time, but my friend, John, lets his stand speak loud and clear. When he agreed to tell me some stories for this book, he said the following:

"The best cure for a juvenile delinquent is a parents' club, but it is best if it is made out of hickory."

John Moore

My granddaughter came into Nana's and Poppy's room one morning at 6:00 am and said, "Poppa, wake up! "He said, "Why?" "I need my purple butterfly dress down and I can't reach it because my knees are not high enough."

Diana Moore

Poppy was getting dressed and Savannah said, "Poppa, you have a bug on your back. "He said, "No it is just a mole." Savannah shouted, "Oh my! I hate moles. I don't like moles on me, they will eat you!"

Diane Moore

Chapter 4

It had rained very hard one night and a posthole that had been dug for a new fence had filled with water. Little Johnny, the four-year-old son of the owner, who happened to be a preacher, had gone outside to play in the yard. In a few minutes, his mama went to check on little Johnny. What she saw shocked her. Her sweet little boy was shoving the newly born kittens in the hole of water. His mother screamed, Johnny, what are you doing?" "I'm playing preacher and I am baptizing these kittens!"

Charles Freeman

I was teaching a fifth grade unit on farm life to city children in Asheville, North Carolina. Growing up on a farm in Kentucky, I decided these city children needed to know some things about farm life. I assigned two boys to draw a cow and place it on the bulletin board. When they finished, I checked on their work and thanked them for doing such a good job with the cow. A while later, the principal came in and said, "Do all the cows in Kentucky have five tits?"

Dr. J. Terry Hall

An old man was listening to the news as they were talking about LGBT and that they have a right to be whatever gender they decide. The old man shook his head and said, "If I could have a dollar for every gender there is in this world, I would have two dollars and a bunch of counterfeits!

Ben F. Hall

My mother-in-law was a wonderful Christian lady, but she would never admit that she was wrong. This following tale is an example.

One bright sunny day my wife and I were taking her to yard sales; she loved to look for treasures. As I was holding the door for her to get in, she spied a spider on the window. She said, "Oh my! There's a Black Widow Spider!" I looked and said, "No, that spider has a white spot on it's back, the black widow spider has a red spot on it's back." Never to be wrong she said, "It turns red when it gets mad."

Dr. J. Terry Hall

Several years ago, my brother-in-law bought a motor bike and my wife and I were in his back yard, watching him ride it around the yard. My wife has never been the kind of girl who would dare to ride a motor bike, but we convinced her to get on the bike. We showed her how to use the throttle and she was on her way, riding in circles around the yard. As she passed us she yelled, "Where's the brake?!She went around again and yelled, "Where's the brake?!We were bent over laughing but managed to say on the fourth time around," Let go of the throttle! She did and came to a stop. For some reason, that was the end of her motor bike riding.

Dr. J. Terry Hall

After retiring from Asheville City Schools, my wife and I moved to Bowling Green, Kentucky where I was hired as Assistant Principal of an elementary school. I loved working at Warren Elementary and especially with the principal, Bea Isable. We also had a custodian who loved to play pranks on others. One day he came into my office about something and I was ready for him. As he turned to leave I was standing at the door and patted him on the back. I stepped out into the hallway and followed him. All of a sudden, several children started kicking him. He yelled, "What are you doing?!" Then, one of the children reached up and pulled a sticky note pad off his back. It said, "KICK ME". He looked back to see me bent over laughing and said, "You just wait!"

Dr. J. Terry Hall

One day, I was in a grocery store and observed a big fat man bent over, getting something off a bottom shelf. When he bent over, half of his butt was showing. Another man, who was also noticing the man looked at me and said, "If I had a crack that big I would put putty in it."

Dr. J. Terry Hall

For several years, I "filled in" for the preacher at Candler Church of Christ. One Sunday morning I pulled my red pickup truck up in front of the church building. One of the small children, who was standing there looked up at his daddy and said, "Jesus is here, we can go inside now." wow! After an introduction like that, what was I going to say?"

Dr. J. Terry Hall

Another memory at Candler went something like this: There was a fellow who always went to sleep during my lessons. It never failed, he would go to sleep as soon as I started and wake up as soon as I finished. Finally, I had had enough and about half way through my lesson, I made a point and slammed my hard-backed Bible down on the roster. The man jumped to his feet, wide-eyed and awake. The following Sunday he once again went to sleep.

Dr. Terry Hall

Another Candler story was when a woman, whose name will remain unknown, got up and went to the restroom during one of my lessons. When she came back, she had a long strip of toilet paper hanging all the way to the floor. It had caught in her panties when she pulled up her clothes. One of the other ladies told her about it.

Dr. J. Terry Hall

During my college days at Lindsey Wilson College, I received a letter from home. In the letter, my mother said it would be nice if I would write a letter to my great aunt who was getting on up in years. Mother went on to say," "You know Susan is old and her mind isn't what it used to be and I believe she would appreciate getting a letter from you."

"Love mother."

I always tried to do what my mother asked so I wrote Aunt Susan a letter, telling her that I loved her. The problem was that I got the two letters mixed up I sent Aunt Susan mother's letter and Aunt Susan's letter to my mother. And I was a college student?

Dr. J. Terry Hall

After Patricia and I married, the big day came when she was going to cook a meal for my parents. To say the least, she was a bit nervous, being newly married and all. I don't remember what she had prepared, but it was wonderful. During the meal, Mother got up to get something out of the refrigerator. When she opened the door, she laughed. Sitting beside the milk was a package of toilet paper. After everybody had a good laugh, Patricia said, "It should be a cool wipe." Everybody laughed and from that point on the stress was over.

Dr. J. Terry Hall

In my younger days, I was "horse crazy." From the earliest time I can remember, I have always loved horses. The first year I began teaching, the first thing I bought was a used Corvair and a used horse.

The second summer I was invited to attend a horse show held at a stable in a local city park. I arrived late due to some problem and could not find a parking place. Everyone was standing around the ring watching the horses and riders so I didn't want to ask anyone where to park.

I noticed an area close to the ring and wondered why no one had parked their car in that area. I thought I had it made; a place to park and no one around me. Little did I know that those high weeds covered a ditch about 2 feet deep. When I pulled in to park, my car lay flat on the ground. I thought, "What do I do now?" After the show ended, about eight men lifted my Corvair off the ground and back onto the road. Even a tow truck could not have lifted my car out of the ditch. It was nice of those men to help me. Believe me, from that time until the present, I am very selective where I park my car.

Dr. Judy Pierce

Speaking of show horses, I have a male friend who also loves horse shows. Some years ago, I became actively involved in the city's horse show by financially supporting the trophy in the Equestrian Championship class. Other horse lovers supported the class financially with halters and a trainer's purse. At the end of the class, a small group of supporters get to walk into the ring and present these items to the winner. A photographer always takes a photograph of the group with the winner of the class. I asked my friend if he would hold my purse while I walked into the ring for the presentation and photograph. Once the group was assembled in the ring, I looked around and he was right behind me holding my purse. I did a double-take and laughed myself silly! And, to this day, I have a picture of the group with my friend grinning like a opossum.

Dr. Judy Pierce

Chapter 5

When I was a small boy, I used to go to the movies. In our small town, there was only two showings to choose from. I was so excited about going that I was the first one out the door. My grandpa was always chewing on a toothpick and on the way to the car he had gotten the toothpick stuck in his throat. Everyone was running around all excited about grandpa. I started crying hysterically. My mom said, "Don't worry son, he will be OK." I looked up through tear-stained eyes and said, "I'm not worried about grandpa, I'm sad because I might miss the beginning of the movie." I had my priorities even at a young age.

Paul and Cameron Lowe

When I turned 13 years old, I got a job working on an oil rig in west Texas. An old man by the name of something, but everybody called him "Happy," was my boss. One hot summer west Texas day, "Happy" told me take the huge drilling rig back to the shop. Being only thirteen years old, I didn't even drive a car much less a big oil rig. But whatever "Happy" told me to do I did it to the best of my ability. The rig had a hand emergency brake. I did not know about the brake and didn't release it. About half way to the shop the cab filled up with smoke and a fire broke out under the rig. I jumped out slid under the rig and began throwing dirt and sand on the fire. After the fire was under control, I released the hand brake and drove it on the shop. A boy grows up fast in west Texas.

Ken Cone

Many years ago, I was showing my horse at a show about 100 miles from my home town in West Virginia. The owner of the stable, Mr. Sunday, where I boarded my horse, had a horse trailer and agreed to take my horse along with his son's horse to the show. The show ended about 11:00 p.m. By the time we packed up the gear and loaded the horses into the trailer, it was about midnight when we started home.

Mother and I were following behind the trailer in my Corvair, when suddenly the fan belt decided to come off. The red engine light came on and was blinking. That was one negative thing about owning a Corvair, the fan belt came off whenever it decided to do so. Mother said, "Don't you think we better stop and fix the fan belt?" I said, "Mother, it is nearly 2:00 am and we are out in the middle of nowhere." We are about 20 miles from home so I am not stopping." There was no way I could contact Mr. Sunday to let him know of our trouble. Cell phones did not exist. Well, we made it home and I will tell you, steam was coming out of that engine like the steam from the smoke stack of a train. I thought sure that the engine was shot. The next morning, someone put on a fan belt and when I turned the engine, it started like a dream.

Dr. Judy Pierce

I once heard about this mountain boy who fell head over heels in love with a girl down the road a mite. He would come over to her house and they would sit on the front porch in the swing and talk and talk and hug and kiss for hours on end. One sunny day, so the story goes, he came by to see the love of his young life and finally as he was getting ready to leave, he took her beautiful face in his hand sand slowly kissed her sweet lips as he tenderly told her that his love was so strong that he would climb the tallest mountain and swim the deepest sea to get back to see her again. He got up to leave and said, "I will be back to see you next Saturday if it don't rain."

Dr. J. Terry Hall

In 1903 a baby was born. This was the ninth baby born to this woman. Every two years like clockwork, Doctor Billy Richardson, the country doctor, would be sent for to come and assist with bringing a newborn into the world. Dr. Richardson would take his black doctor's bag, saddle up his horse, and ride down to the Cumberland River in the Elbow Community to deliver the child. Sometimes he would have to stay for several days before the baby decided to join the family. During this time, all the other children would accept the doctor being there just as one of the family.

One day, as the story goes,13 year old Elizabeth was asked if she remembered something or another and she thought for a minute before saying, "I can't remember, I guess I was still in Dr. Richardson's little black bag.

Dr. J. Terry Hall

In the North Carolina mountains where I live, it is not uncommon to hear about the authorities finding a moonshine still way back in the hills. Nowadays, they are more likely to find pot. But this tale was told by a relative who lived in the mountains of Polk County.

We will call the old man, Ben. Ben went walking in the mountains with his old friend Joe. During their walk Ben spied something shiny at the base of a stump. Walking over, Ben pulled out a gallon jug of moonshine. Looking at Joe, Ben said, "I've had me a hankering to try a sip of moonshine and this here is my chance." Joe said, "Wait a minute

Ben. If you drink moonshine before it is mellow it could kill you. You don't want to die now do you." Ben said, "I shore ain't ready to die Joe so I guess I better leave it be." They walked on down the mountain and home.

Later that day, Ben got to thinking about that jug of moonshine and decided to go back up there and bring the jug back home. As he approached the stump, he heard Joe said, Mellooo, Mellooo.

Dr. J. Terry Hall

Dear Heavenly Father.

So far today I have done all right. I haven't gossiped or lost my temper. I haven't been greedy, grumpy, nasty or self centered.

I'm really happy about that so far, but in a few minutes I'm going to be getting out of bed and then I'm going to need a lot of help. Thank You, Amen

Diana Moore

These were found in church bulletins:

For those of you who have children and don't know it, we have a nursery downstairs.

Diana Moore

The Weight Watchers will meet downstairs. Please use the double doors at the rear entrance.

Diana Moore

The doctor's six year old Judy answered the door. Is the doctor home? "No, Ma'am," said the child, "he is out performing a appendectomy."

"My, that's a big word for such a little girl. Do you know what it means?" It means $3,500 and that doesn't include the anesthetist."

Diana Moore

An irate customer called the newspaper and loudly demanded, WHERE is my SUNDAY paper? "Madam, said the newspaper employee, today is Saturday. The Sunday paper will not be delivered until tomorrow, on Sunday."

There was a long pause followed by a ray of recognition as she muttered, "Well, that explains why there was no one at church either."

Diana Moore

An elderly woman died last month and had never married, She requested that no male pallbearers be used. In her handwritten instructions for her memorial service, she wrote, "They wouldn't take me out while I was alive so I don't want them to take me out when I'm dead."

Diana Moore

One evening our young son Andrew was playing in the bathtub and pretending to be baptizing his Power Ranger action figure. He said, "Now I baptize you in the name of God and Jesus, with liberty and justice for all."

Diana Moore

When I was growing up in south central Kentucky, Blue Grass music was the music of choice. This was back before television and the choices were listening to the Grand Old Opera or making your own music.

The tenant farmer on my grandparents farm was Earl Gearlds. Earl came from down on the Cumberland River where almost everyone learned to play a musical instrument shortly after they learned to walk. Every Saturday night four or five of them would drive the ten miles to Earl's house and pick, sang and dance. They had some of the best cloggers anywhere around. Of course, being a young boy growing up listening to this music, I loved to go down to Earl's place and join in. I never learned to play an instrument, but I did learn to clog. For those who did not have the advantage of growing up clogging, clogging is a very fast dance where the dancer's feet is moving to the beat of the music, but the head is nearly still.

That's enough of the background. The story goes like this: There used to be a house near where I live in North Carolina where people would meet and play Blue Grass music every Thursday night. Of course, most Thursday nights I would be sitting on the front row or on the dance floor. When my grandson, Dakota turned fourteen, I decided to take him to the dance and show him what he had been missing. It didn't take me long to get on the floor and show Dakota how Pap-Paw could clog. As others joined in, I could hear Dakota yelling from the crowd, "Sit down Pap-Paw, you'll break another hip!" I laughed so hard I couldn't dance.

Dr. J. Terry Hall

My friends know that I sing or play the piano for weddings and funerals when requested by the family. The first year that I began teaching, I was moved from one school to another school due to low enrollment. The Friday afternoon prior to Labor Day weekend, I drove out to my new school to meet the children. It was a good meeting and after school I had to get ready to sing for a friend's wedding about 150 miles from Charleston. I was concerned about taking my Corvair and my grandmother did not think it was a good idea since the fan belt came off at any time, and about 100 miles of the highway was desolate. I was perplexed, I didn't have any idea how I was going to get to this wedding. I called Jackie, a friend of the bride and advised her that I had no way to get to the wedding. Jackie advised me that she would work it out.

On Saturday morning, the telephone rang, and a member of the bride's family, Thomas advised me that they would pick me up and possibly bring me home. So I packed an overnight bag not knowing if I would be coming home that night or on Sunday.

Thomas and his family picked me up about noon and we drove to a beautiful part of West Virginia. The trees in the mountains were beginning to change color and it was a gorgeous day.

About 6:15 p.m., we arrived at this beautiful one room country church about 45 minutes prior to the beginning of the wedding. I began to play the piano about 6:30 p.m. as the wedding was scheduled to begin about 7:00 p.m. The preacher, best man, and groom walked down to the front of the church about 6:55 p.m. I stopped playing and looked toward the back of the church for the bride in order to begin playing the wedding march. There was a slight problem; there was no bride. I kept playing the wedding music for another 15minutes, still no bride. That little church was packed with people with no standing room. Everyone About 45 minutes later, the bride arrived. I began to look at each other including the preacher, the groom, the best man, and me. I just kept playing repeating some of the songs. Where was the bride? We didn't have cell phones in those days and there were no telephones in the church, so there was no way of finding out what was going wrong with the bride. I kept playing the same songs over and over. There is just so many times that songs can be played until people get tired hearing them. led the wedding march as the bride walked down the short aisle to meet her future husband. She was a beautiful bride. The reception was held at Jackie's home. Her parents had sold their house and were moving to Florida. All the furniture was gone except the kitchen table. Their bags were packed and they were ready to head to Florida that night. After a brief reception, Thomas and his family drove me home. No one to this day knows why the bride was 45 minutes late for her own wedding.

Dr. Judy Pierce

Chapter 6

Jack Waters had a full mane of wild long hair, tattoos everywhere and a face tattooed with piercings. He was a fanatic skater and was never seen without his skateboard. Jack had a real affinity for LSD and probably took one too many acid trips.

Jack used to live with his girlfriend, Andrea along with her mother, Kate. Jack and Andrea had a bad break-up and Kate banned Jack from the house. Sometimes later, I received a call reporting a breaking and entering in progress at the Waters residence. I was on bicycle patrol at the time and was literally a half block from the house. Just as I rode up, I saw Jack climbing out of Andrea's window carrying his trusty skateboard. He looked at me pedaling toward him with a look of terror on his face.

Jack took off running into the woods that went uphill behind the house still gripping his skateboard. I took up my bicycle under my arm and pursued him into the woods. At the top of the hill, there was a road and old Jack threw that skateboard down on the street, jumped on it and started kicking for all his life, looking back at me with the most horrifying facial expression.

When I got to the road, I mounted the bike and started racing toward Jack closing the gap between us at brake neck speed. In short order, I crashed into Jack and it was like one of those cartoons with a cloud of dust with feet, hands, skateboard and bicycle tires sticking out. Jack went absolutely crazy, screaming and freaking out like a maniac. I got him hooked up in cuffs and transferred to a marked car, him flipping out the whole time. I got him all the way to the jail and he never did calm down. I couldn't figure out what was tearing at him so bad.

I got him processed and on the way back got a call that Kate wanted to see me at her house. When I got there, she invited me in for coffee with a big grin on her face, saying that she had a story to tell me that I just had to hear. Apparently, during that last week or so he had lived there, Jack suffered from terrifying nightmares from which he would awaken screaming. According to Kate, Jack told her that during these nightmares, he dreamed he was on his skateboard being chased by Officer Ribley on that dammed bike," and when I caught up with him and crashed into him he would wake up screaming in terror. For me, it gave new meaning to the phrase, "I'm your worst nightmare."

Detective Lee Ribley

We responded to a report of an armed robbery at Taco Bell where victims described a tall man, later identified as Joe Taylor, brandishing a butcher knife and wearing a white t-shirt over his head, tied at the top and with two eye holes cut out. The suspect fled the scene just before the first units arrived, but officers heading in the direction of the suspect's last known location located the t-shirt in the roadway. Despite his makeshift mask, restaurant employees were able to pick the suspect out of a photo lineup because during the robbery, he pulled his mask to the left and right trying to hide his face. The employees who were much shorter than the suspect could see under it. The same suspect was also under investigation for another armed robbery at a nearby convenience store.

Detective David Mitchell and Officer Hill White and I searched the suspect's house where we located some good evidence against Joe including clothing matching the eye witnesses description and a large bag of money. Just then, from the bathroom, Hill started cheering, for there on the counter, he had discovered the mother of all incriminating evidence: a pair of scissors and two small circles of cloth that perfectly matched the t-shirt eyeholes. I looked at Joe and said, "If the eye holes fit, you can't acquit!"

Detective Lee Ribley

I am sure everyone has heard of candlelight weddings. Well, I have really participated in a real candlelight wedding. One of my college friends Janet, asked me to sing at her wedding. I agreed to do so because she had helped me with several assignments in a elementary mathematics class we were taking that semester. She was majoring in secondary education with an emphasis of mathematics and was a whiz. Janet and her boyfriend were planning to marry in February about three months before graduation. They planned to move from West Virginia after graduation and did not want to wait until that time to marry.

Now people in Charleston, West Virginia know that from November through March there is usually a large amount of snowfall. Well, you guessed it! The night of the wedding rehearsal, there had been a big snowfall that day. My boyfriend, Sonny decided to go with me to the church because the roads were icy and slick. We poked along this country road at about fifteen miles an hour. We could hardly see the road much less find the church. It was pitch dark and you could not see your hand in front of your face. Suddenly, we came upon a car in front of us driving even slower than we were down the road. I recognized Janet's car and we followed her taillights to the church.

Well, the one room church was located down an embankment. People had to park their cars at the top of the hill and walk down the embankment to get to the front door. There were no steps down the hill. The only light was the one over the front door and a concrete step before entering the church. Inside the church, in the center of the room, there was a very large black potbelly stove, a few benches, a pulpit, an out-of-tune piano and one overhead light in the church. I asked, "Janet, are you going to have music as you march down the isle?" She replied, "Yes, we are going to have a record player and a recording of the wedding march." One of the members of the church, John, suggested we rehearse with the music. I began by singing "The Lord's Prayer." When John turned on the record player, it blew out the overhead light. He said, "I don't think the record player will work tonight. We will work on this problem in the morning and everything will be working smoothly by tomorrow night." Janet said, "It will be OK." Well, by the next evening there was more snow piled on top of the snow on the ground. Sonny and I arrived a little early at the church because I wanted to find out if we were going to have a light and enough electricity to play the wedding march. He had to carry me down the embankment because of the snow. The little church was nice and warm as John had arrived early and built a fire in the stove. People began filling the benches and at 7:00 p.m., I began singing my song. After my song, I waited for the bridal march. You see, I was also the maid of honor. Well, you guessed it, the record player would not work and the overhead light went out. Thank goodness there were some candles handy in the church. The people could see to light them by the light coming from the pot bellied stove. When Janet was ready to walk down the isle everybody hummed the wedding march.

Dr. Judy Pierce

This is not a funny story, but I felt compelled to include it in my book.

It was a cool Florida evening as my partner for the night shift and I were on duty in a marked unit with the Florida Highway patrol. We were cruising east bound on Interstate 4 in Seminole County near Orlando. It was around 2:00 a.m. And so far it had a relatively quiet evening. I was the passenger and my partner was the driver.

I-4 was pretty desolate then, and we observed a vehicle in front of us that was driving at a very high rate of speed, in the same direction as we were traveling. We followed it for a short period of time and clocked it against our speedometer around 85 miles per hour in a 65 mph zone. We decided to initiate a traffic stop based on unlawful speed.

My partner activated lights and we gained on the offender. To our surprise, rather than a traditional stop on the right side of the highway, the driver pulled into the grass median, although there was no traffic preventing him from a traditional stop. The area in the middle of the interstate was extremely dark and unlit as may be expected on a multi-lane rural highway.

We stopped the patrol vehicle about thirty feet behind the offender. I got out and approached the driver's side of the vehicle while observing multiple occupants in the vehicle. I had no portable radio as these were in limited supply at the time, and no way to contact my partner.

The driver rolled down his window and I observed six male occupants, three in the front and three in the rear. I was friendly and polite also aware that my partner and I were outnumbered. I asked the driver for his license, proof of insurance and registration. While doing so, I noticed a very large roll of cash in the pocket of his shirt, which I ignored.

The driver told me he did not have any of the documentation that I requested, with an unsupported story as requested, with an unsupported story as to why. It made no sense. I asked him for his name and date of birth. He did provide the information and I noted it in my handbook. I walked backwards to my patrol vehicle in the grass and dirt and advised my partner of my observations.

The offenders vehicle was well lighted with our headlights. While waiting for my partner to run a radio check, I re-approached the driver's side and engaged in light conservation such as, "We will have you out of here in just a minute. Hey, where did that wad of cash?" He told me that he and his friends sold several things at a fairground which was an all cash business. We talked about that and I commented, "Maybe I am in the wrong business.! "After being law enforcement as long as I have, you get a sense when something didn't sound right. I had that sense.

All of a sudden, my partner shut off the flashing lights and the headlights, leaving me in total darkness. I knew something was very wrong. I told the group that we had been having trouble with our battery and I would go see what was going wrong. I put my hand on my firearm and walked backward in total darkness, at one point I could not ever see the patrol car.

When I got to the window I asked, "What's going on? "My partner told me that the driver was wanted for murder and he had called for back-up!"

I removed my duty weapon and held it beside my leg and in the dark, As I walked back to the offender' car. I told him that I was right, and the battery was about to crap out so we are going to write him a warning and let him go. He was good with that; his lucky day. We talked for about ten minutes. We talked for some time giving the back-up officers time to respond. All of a sudden, I saw the Calvary approaching. Lights and sirens coming toward us. We surrounded the vehicle and ordered everyone out. The place was all lit up now with officers everywhere as we commanded them to get on the ground and placed them under arrest

A search of the vehicle disclosed several handguns under the seat and a police radio. Why they did not run when we called for back-up no one will ever know.

After we all caught our breath and things were stabilized, I asked my young partner why he turned off the lights and left to in the dark? He replied, "Sergeant, if I had left my lights on you would have been an easy target and if it had come to a gun fight, you would not have had a chance.

I will be forever grateful. Even now, after twenty years, I refer to him as the one who saved my life.

"There is no such thing as a routine traffic stop or a routine call. Just ask any policeman or policewoman.

A big Thank You goes out to all police who put their lives on the line every time they walk out the door.

Harvey Moore

Chapter 7

The first year I taught school, three friends, Jolene, Wanda, Susie and I decided that we were going skiing which was something that none of us had done.

It was February and there was snow on the ground when we left Charleston on that Friday evening. We drove about two hours and it began to snow in the mountains. We also noticed a red car had been following us since we had left Charleston.

We stopped to get some gas and I told my friend, Jolene, who was driving, that we needed chains on our rear tires. She agreed and asked the young man at the gas station if he would put the chains on the rear tires. I watched him put on the chains and told Jolene that he had put them on crooked. The gas station was about to close and the young man said that, "he didn't have the time to change them. "At that point, we saw the red car again.

In order to save time, the group decided to drive over the mountains to the state park instead of through the valley. About midnight, we were going up a hill when the chain on the driver's side began to clank, clank, clank. I said, "Jolene, let's stop the car and see if we can do anything with the chain." Jolene stopped the car. We got out, and, sure enough, the chain was crooked and trying to get off the tire. I tried to remove the chain, but it was so tight on the tire that I could not get my fingers between the chain and the tire.

The snow was coming down so fast that we could barely see the front end of the car. We drove on up the hill about fifteen miles an hour. About ten minutes later, we heard the chain on the other tire, go clank, clank clank. We just drove on.

The snow was so blinding that we could not see the front end of the car. The car began sliding down the hill. Little did we know that a semi was jack-knifed in the middle of the road. The grill on Jolene's car slid into the right front bumper of the semi. The driver of the semi got out and helped us see if there was any damage. He told us that he had been sitting there for more than four hours and had not seen a soul. He radioed for help, but could not seemed to rouse anyone. So we were in a fix and didn't know what we were going to do.

The storm had almost turned into a blizzard and we could not get any help. I mentioned the red car that had followed us from Charleston. I said, "Maybe they took the same route as we did."

Well, speaking of luck, a few minutes later, here came the red car. The boys stopped to see if they could help. They got out and, with the help of the truck driver, cleared away enough of the snow so they could get around the semi. It was decided that Jolene and I would stay in the semi, while the driver, Wanda and Susan would go to the lodge to get help. Jolene and I climbed into the semi to get warm. Little did we know that the semi was resting on the side of the mountain! The engine began making a funny noise; it would get loud and then soft! Loud and then soft. It kept doing this throughout the night. The snow kept falling and we wondered if we would ever be found.

At 7:00 a.m. the next morning, the state police just happened by and saw the accident. The officers had to clear the road so that they and other cars could get around the semi. They contacted a tow trunk on their radio to come and get Jolene's car. Meanwhile, the officers packed our luggage in the police car and were taken to the lodge. Once we arrived, here came Wanda and Susan, running down the steps. Wanda said," We could not get any help because everyone was drunk.

As it turned out, there was so much snow that we could not go skiing. The lodge had to close the ski slope because of the blizzard. That evening, some of the people decided to have a big dance. We cleared the big room of tables and chairs and began dancing the polka. What fun!

On Sunday the man with the tow truck company brought Jolene's car to the lodge. It was not damaged and we counted our blessings. We packed our luggage in the trunk of the car. When Wanda and I opened the back door, the gallon of coffee and the fruit was in the floor and had frozen. Wanda and I were riding in the back seat and could not put our feet on the floor all the way back home. That was the longest trip home in history.

Dr. Judy Pierce

When I was in high school, there was this boy who lived down on the Cumberland River by the name of Joe. Joe was always claiming something or the other had happened and most of us took it with a grain of salt. He had bought a rain gauge and was always bragging about how much rain he had received at his house. One day, I decided to play a trick on Joe. After dark, I slipped down to his house and poured water in his rain gauge. I poured enough in to measure four inches of rain. The next morning he came to school and told everybody that he had four inches of rain at his house. We would tell him that we didn't get a drop at our house. The next night; I did the same thing with four inches of water in the gauge. Well, that continued for five days, no one ever accused Joe of being to bright. After five days, he stopped in the middle of his story and said, "Have you guys been to my house?" Everybody broke out laughing as Joe stood there and just shook his head.

Dr. J. Terry Hall

My wife's daddy used to drink a mite of moonshine when he was young as most folks did in his neck-of-the-woods. Well, one night he and his drinking buddy decided to drive up the mountain over in what was called Dark Corner on the South Carolina line. "When they got to the moonshine still, they told the moonshiner that they wanted five gallons of moonshine. He gave it to them and they paid the man.

As they went back down the mountain, they had to cross a creek. Well, as fate would have it, their car died right in the middle of the creek and they could not get it started. As they sat there trying to decide what to do, a big black car came to the creek on the other side of the road, going up the mountain. Ben told them that his car had died and he needed to be pulled out of the creek for the black car to get through. As the black car continued on up the mountain, Ben turned to his friend and said, "John, ain't nobody around here could afford a car like that. I bet they were revenuers. "Well, they got their car started and continued on down the mountain.

A few days later, they met the moonshiner on the street in Tryon, NC and told him about the big black car. He said," I shore am glad you had already gone; they were revenuers and I had just sold you the last moonshine I had on my place.

Dr. J, Terry Hall

When I was working at Vance Elementary School in Asheville, North Carolina as Assistant Principal, I was observing a kindergarten class when a five-year-old boy asked to go to the restroom. The teacher allowed him to go and while he was gone, I finished my observation and started up the hallway. About halfway up the hallway, I met the little boy. He was singing a song as he walked which was a popular commercial at that time. He was singing:

"POP-POP FIZZ-FIZZ, OH WHAT A RELIEF IT IS."

Five year old children are wonderful.

Dr. J. Terry Hall

Reagan in my second-grade class. I would get to school early and so would Reagan. He was bored waiting for the other students to arrive, so he asked if he could be my "helper" in the classroom. So before school started, I would have him trim a friend of mine who worked for a government department in Raleigh, NC. He was interviewing for a secretary and she was asked, to fill out a form. At the bottom of the form she read, "Print your name here." When she turned in the form, on the signature line, she had printed, "Your name here." She didn't get the job.

Don Carter

While working on my doctorate in West Virginia, one of my responsibilities as a graduate student was to place students in local schools for their student teaching. I held several seminars with the student teachers prior to and during their student teaching experience. Some of the things we had discussed in-depth were lesson planning, classroom management, and professional dress. The university did not allow student teachers to wear tennis shoes, sandals, or jeans.

One of my students, Maddie was a beautiful young lady who always looked like "she had just stepped out of Vogue." She probably spent two hours every morning just "putting on her face" before touching her hair. Never was there a hair out of place. Her clothes were exquisite and beautiful. Maddie was placed into a third-grade classroom for her last three weeks of her student teaching.

One day I received a call from her principal. She asked that I come to school to have a conference with a concerned parent, the cooperating field teacher and Maddie. I agreed and at the appointed time the next day, I met with the group. When I entered the classroom, I noticed Maddie had cut her hair. It looked nice and Maddie was dressed as her usual self. When I asked the mother about her concern, she said, "I came home from work yesterday and found my little girl, Susie had put a bowl on her head, took a pair of scissors and cut her hair. Not only that, she had makeup smeared all over her face and used up all of my perfume. I asked Susie why she had done that and she said, "Miss Mattie cut her hair and I wanted to look and smell just like her."

Mattie apologized and then realized that she had been a role model for Susie. She learned that children do and say at home what the teacher does at school; how teachers dress and how they talk. I am sure that was a good lesson for Mattie. Thank goodness it was her last week of student teaching.

Dr. Judy Pierce

One year I had the principal's son, everyone's pencils so we would not have to do this during class. I asked him not to mention he was my "helper" because I knew I would have a room full of "helpers" before class every morning.

One day another student asked, "How come when we go home every day, our pencils are all broken, but when we come back in the morning, they are all trimmed again? "Reagan kept mum, and I said,

"Oh, we have a little pencil fairy that comes in every night and sharpens them so they are ready for us the next morning! "A few minutes later Reagan came up quietly and whispered in my ear, "I'd just as soon that you didn't call me a fairy!" I cracked up in class and all the students wanted to know what was so funny!

Elaine Burgess

We had a family from Nicaragua that came to our church to start a Spanish ministry because of the growing number of Latinos in our town. The two boys were beginning to learn English very well.

I picked up the boys after school one day and took them home with me for awhile. As I was fixing them a snack, the little kindergarten boy said, Lane, Lane, you've got a big butt." Tickled, but trying to keep a straight face, I said," Santy, you shouldn't say that!" "Oh," he said, "Should I have said bottom?"

Elaine Burgess

Chapter 8

When I was very young, I was given a book about weather. Ever since I read that book, I have been fascinated with weather. So I turned into a weather forecaster o'sorts. My hobby is trying to outdo weather forecasters. Most times I say, it's not going to rain or snow any more when they say it will and I'm often correct by using common sense and looking at the direction the weather is moving on radar.

My funniest forecast was right after we got married. One day at work I heard about three guys who were going to play golf when they get off work. I told them that if they did that, they would get far away from the club house on the third fairway and it would rain on them. I was teasing and guessing, but said it seriously, and did think it might rain. The next day they came to me quite upset. In a teasing way they said, "Jones, you SOB, we got on the third fairway and it came a down pour and we got soaked!" I simply said, "Well next time maybe you will listen to me."

A few years later, the guys came and asked me what the snow officials were predicting. I said, "Well all I can say is, it could be a record-setting blizzard." This was based on a low and dropping barometric pressure, a NE wind and a halo around the dim sun. The next day it started snowing and they had closed the office, that Wednesday afternoon. I barely made it to the garage as my wife held open the garage door so I didn't have to slow down. Authorities shut down the entire state of Indiana to all traffic. All trucks and traffic were stopped at the border. Everything remained shut down Thursday and Friday. The official total was fifteen inches at the airport, but the drifts were horrific with some of them being four feet. A t-shirt came out saying, I survived the blizzard of 77-78.

Steve Jones

In 1969, I worked at a place full of crazy people. My immediate boss fought in Korea. I think the experience made him paranoid. We would often talk about the war and it's horrors. He told me once that the trunk of his car was full of live hand-grenades. To that I said, "Don't you realize that if someone rear-ended you, that you would blow up half the city?" The look on his face was priceless. Another story by him was that once their squad was on patrol, and they didn't want to be discovered. Suddenly they heard enemy troops, and they all dove for cover. It was a Japanese patrol. The problem was, he found himself in a latrine pit. No, he didn't move. The patrol passed without incident. But all the way back to camp, no one got near him.

Steve Jones

I worked with the Department of Education for two years. During my tenure, I visited school districts throughout the state and met with teachers and administrators. One of the most interesting districts was where the State Department was located and where I was born and raised. While growing up, I heard so much about the "Red Light District" in the capital city. I was very naïve and had no clue what that phrase meant until I became an adult. While I was with the State Department, the local County Board of Education decided to build a new school in the "Red Light District." as a result, several brothels were torn down to make room for the new school. The first year the school opened, a new teacher was hired to teach kindergarten. She asked the children to call her Mrs. June. One day the teacher came to school not feeling well. The teacher said, "Boys and girls, I want you to be on your very best behavior today because Mrs. June does not feel well." A little boy who was beside himself, kept waving his hand frantically. Finally, the teacher called on the little boy. He said, "Mrs. June if you don't feel well why don't you hire a prostitute?" The teacher had to leave the room to laugh at what the child had remarked.

Dr. Judy Pierce

While I worked with the Department of Education one of my friends, Betty was a University Supervisor of student teachers. One of Betty's student teachers got a wonderful job teaching third grade in a district close to the university. One day Betty received an alarming call from the new teacher, Julie. Of course, Betty was wondering what was wrong. It was the end of the first month of school for Julie and everything seemed to be going well for her. Well, Betty agreed to meet with Julie after school at the university.

At the meeting, Julie was very upset. Betty asked Julie how she might help. Julie went on to say that earlier that week, she received a telephone call from the Principal who sounded very upset. She said, "He told me he wanted to see me first thing the next morning in his office, but gave no reason." He did not say good-bye he just hung up the telephone. Well, being a new teacher, I did not sleep much that night wondering what I had done wrong.

The next morning, I walked into the principal's office and found one of my children's mother sitting next to the door. The mother just stared at me. The principal came out of his office and invited the mother and I into his office. Once inside, he closed the door. The principal said, "Mrs. Hugh has complained about the language that you are using in the classroom." I was dumbfounded, and said, "I do not use bad English in the classroom. Grammar is very important to me."

The mother spoke up and said, "It is not bad English you are using it is bad words." I spoke up and said, "What do you mean, bad words?" The mother said, "Well, my son was sitting at the kitchen table last evening working on his multiplication table while I was preparing dinner and he was saying, "two times two the son of a bitch equals four. "I was startled that a third grade child would be using such language. When I asked him where he had heard such language, he said, "That is what my teacher says every time she teaches the multiplication table." I was speechless. Finally, I said, "Oh No, I was saying, "two times two the sum of which equals four. "The mother calmed down, but by the expression on her face, was not very satisfied. Being a highly educated person, she asked, "Who taught you to teach mathematics? Then added," "When adding, you say the sum of which, not multiplication." She stomped out of the principal's office still glaring at me. Meanwhile, the principal advised me to become more familiar with arithmetic because he didn't want any more complaints from that mother because she is very influential in the community.

Dr. Judy Pierce

My son and his wife were playing a name game with their nine-year-old daughter and related this conversation to be placed in my book:

Ben asked Dicey, "Dicey, do you know your full name," to which Dicey quickly answered, "Dicey Riley Hall. "Ben then said, "what is your mama's full name?" Dicey replied, "Kimberly Nicole Hall."

He then asked for his full name to which she replied "Ben Frank Hall. "He then asked, what is your Mam-ma's full name? Dicey replied,

"Mam-ma Patricia Hall. "One to go, what is your pap-paw's full name? Dicey quickly said, "Pap-paw Patricia Hall. Everyone laughed.

Ben and Nickkie Hall

My friends know I love to share stories about the Civil War at various re-enactments in Kentucky. One year I was sharing stories with about six hundred 5th and 6th grade students at a battlefield in eastern Kentucky. One of my friends, Sandy who was also a re-enactor, was telling a story about her son when he was in the second grade. Apparently, his teacher was teaching a unit on animal habitats. The teacher asked the class to think about what it meant to hibernate for the winter. She said, "What would animals do during that time?" After a class discussion she asked, the children to think about two things they would take with them if they hibernated during the winter. After a brief time, Sandy's son raised his hand. The teacher asked him to share his ideas with the class. He said, "I would take a case of beer and a fly swatter with me." The teacher asked, "Why would you take those items with you?" He said, "Well, I am sure I would get thirsty and I could use the fly swatter for entertainment." The teacher had to leave the room to laugh at what the child shared with the class.

Dr. Judy Pierce

Some years ago, on a very cold Saturday before Thanksgiving, three friends and I decided to go horseback riding. One friend, just bought a beautiful palomino gelding named Ed after "Mr. Ed" from the television series. Lisa also owned a horse a big black gelding she called, "The Black. "I owned a colt, but he was not broken to ride. So my other friend, Maxine had to rent our horses for the ride. At any, rate I was on the mounting post ready to mount my horse. Chelsea, moved and I ended up sitting in a pile of horse manure. I got up and mounted Chelsea wearing frozen manure on the seat of my pants. When trying to move with the saddle, it was almost impossible because my pants were glued to it.

We were having a great time riding down the dirt road, when someone suggested we ride on this unmarked trail leading up to the top of the mountain. Well, we were adventuresome on that day so we took off up the side of this mountain. Little did we know that we were on private property. We ended up at a barbed wire fence in the middle of, who knows where, on the mountain.

Well, we had to turn around and find our way back to the dirt road. The only problem was we did not know which way we had come. No one paid any attention to the way we had come because we were having so much fun. I was leading the group down the trail which was the way we thought we had come. Mary was the last rider. Suddenly, her horse bolted and she was thrown. Lisa got off her horse to help Mary get remounted. Mary had somehow hurt her back but she was able to mount Ed. We finally got back to the dirt road. As soon as we reached the dirt road, for some reason, the Black threw Lisa, now Lisa was a heavy set woman, and being thrown from her horse I am sure, was not any fun. Her daughter, Maxine dismounted from her horse and helped Lisa up from the road. Well, Lisa also hurt her back. However she was able to mount her horse. Finally, we had enough of horseback riding for the day and decided to return to the stable. Maxine's horse was full of spirit, just bucking up a storm. He took off with her pulling at the reins, yelling "Whoa, Whoa." Thank goodness the horse finally stopped. I thought sure that Maxine was also going to be thrown, but she wasn't that day. What a day!

Finally, we reached the stable, and I was never so glad to see a barn in my life as I was on that day. I climbed into my car after placing a towel in my car seat because of the frozen manure on my pants. It was a long drive home and not only were my pants frozen, but so was my bottom. Mary and Lisa recovered from sore backs and we went riding again the next weekend. From our experiences that day, one might believe that we were novices at horseback riding. Believe it or not, we had ridden horses for years.

Dr. Judy Pierce

Chapter 9

I was sharing Civil War stories with a group of 5th and 6th grade students in southern Kentucky some years ago. In order to enhance the stories, I wore a Confederate artillery uniform such as they wore during the war. I shared stories about Kentucky during the war along with some scary stories that took place at some of the major battlefields. At the end of the stories, I always give students an opportunity to ask questions. One young boy asked, "Do you enjoy being a man in the war? Did you gey some time away from fighting to come and talk with the class?"

Dr. Judy Pierce

Speaking of sharing stories of the Civil War, one time I was working with a group of fourth grade students at a local elementary school. I was wearing my Confederate artillery uniform such as was worn during the war. I shared story after story about Kentucky's role during the Civil war and how it affected the economy. As usual I gave students opportunity to ask questions. One young boy asked, "How old were you when the Civil War started?" I said, "Do you think I look 140 years old?" He said, "Yes mam."

Dr. Judy Pierce

I am an university professor and often have my undergraduate students work with students at local elementary schools. One year, a principal at one of the schools suggested we have a history museum. My students would choose a historical character, research that individual, and on the day of the museum would come dressed as their character. The fourth grade teachers would work with their children and prepare question to ask my students. Well, one of my students loved Abraham Lincoln and on that day, came early to the elementary school dressed as Lincoln. He word a stove pipe hat, a glued on beard, black pants, a flock coat, and black boots. He even had a glued on mole. None of my students had arrived except Lincoln. Well, we were in the media center arranging tables when a first grade student walked in to get a book. His eyes hot big as saucers and his mouth opened. The little boy said, "Abraham Lincoln." Wow, I was told you were dead. Wait until everyone finds out you are still alive." He hurriedly left the media center.

Dr. Judy Pierce

I heard this story a while back. It seems that there was a preacher walking down the street when he observed a young boy pushing a lawn mower. The preacher asked if the boy's daddy would consider selling the mower as he was looking for one. The boy said, "He just bought a new one, I'll go ask him." The boy came back and told the preacher that his daddy said it was OK. The preacher asked the boy, "Are you sure that the mower will start?" To which the boy assured him that it would. About a week passed and the boy once again came walking by the preacher's house and observed the preacher pulling on the rope to start with sweat running down his brow. He looked up, saw the boy, and said, "You told me that this lawn mower would start and I have been yanking on this rope for an hour." The boy said, "You do have to cuss it to get it to start." The preacher replied, "Son, I am a preacher and it has been years since I cussed. Why, I wouldn't even know how to start. "The young boy and calmly said, "Just keep on jerking on that rope, it'll come back to you."

Dr. J. Terry Hall

One day several years ago, our four year old grandson, Dakota came to Kentucky for a visit while we were living there. The road between Glasgow, Kentucky and Temple Hill, Kentucky, where I was teaching school, was very very crooked and I was driving a little too fast as we rounded a curve. My wife, Patricia said, "Terry honey, slow down! We then heard Dakota from the back seat say, "Pap-paw Terry Honey, slow down!"

Dr. J. Terry Hall

I heard about these boys who were best of friends and did almost everything together. The only thing different was that they went to different church congregations. One went to the Catholic Church and the other to the Church of Christ. One day, one of the boys invited his friend to attend church with him the next Sunday morning. The other boy agreed, but said, "If I go with you to the Catholic Church will you go with me to the Church of Christ church the following Sunday. The boys agreed, but asked each other to explain what the different acts of worship meant.

The next Sunday, They went to the Catholic Church and during the worship the boy from the Church of Christ asked several questions and the other one answered each question. The following Sunday they attended the Church of Christ and the Catholic boy was the one asking the questions. The Church of Christ boy did a wonderful job providing the details of worship. Finally, the preacher walked up to the pulpit, took off his watch, and placed it on the pulpit. The Catholic asked, "What does that mean?" To which the Church of Christ boy responded, "It don't mean a darn thing!"

Dr. J. Terry Hall

My wife's father, Ben Cochran was an expert carpenter. Over forty or more years he worked on many housing projects throughout Henderson County, North Carolina. As a veteran carpenter he realized the danger of children playing around the work-site.

One day there was this young boy, around four years old, who would walk over to the work-site to watch the men work. Ben had told the boy several times to go home and not come back. The boy would leave to only return in a few minutes. Finally, Ben had had it and told the young boy if he came back again he would nail his feet to the floor. Well, you guessed it. In about fifteen minutes Ben turned around and the boy was right in the way. Ben reached for a hammer and a nail and taking the boy's foot nailed the nail through the sole of the boy's shoe. The boy went ballistic, and in a minute or two, Ben pulled the nail out and the boy ran home and stayed.

Like I said, this was several years ago. Today, he would most likely have been looking at a law suit. Back then, they believed it took a whole community to raise a child.

Ben Cochran

My cousin, Judy lived in Kentucky where I grew up. She was about three years old. It was about the middle of December when my mother turned to Judy's mother and said, "Well, Old Santa is right around the corner. "In a few minutes they missed Judy. After searching the house from top to bottom they went outside looking and calling Judy's name. As they were about to panic, Judy came from around the house. She looked up at her mother and asked, "Which corner?"

Dr. J. Terry Hall

Another story about my cousin Judy was how she always made everybody laugh. One thing I remember was when she was learning to talk pretty well and the movie "101 Dalmatians was playing at the one theater in Tompkinsville, Kentucky. The adults would ask Judy what movie she had seen? She would always answer, "101 Damn Nations and everybody would laugh.

Dr. J. Terry Hall

I had four of my front teeth pulled out and my five and nine year old grandchildren asked about my teeth. I had them sit down on a footstool as I stood above them. I told them a story. "Last night I was talking around the house when I saw a big Bat flying by me. All of a sudden that bat flew down and bit me on the arm. This morning, when I woke up I looked like this. I leaned toward them, rolled by eyes upward, and opened my mouth. As I said, "I AM DRACULA!"

Dr. J. Terry Hall

If you have seen me at my gun or craft shows you know, I have a uniform which I wear at each show. It consist of a red shirt and a black cowboy hat. Such an outfit makes it easier for folks to find me as they look around the arena.

The cowboy hat which I bought was the only one that I liked so I bought it, although it was a size to little. At one of my shows, a man walked up to me and told me that my hat was to small. Just for the fun of it I replied, "The hat used to fit, but after I became an author I got the "Big Head" and it became to small. "The customer said, Yea Right!"

Dr. J. Terry Hall

My wife, Patricia loves to go to yard sales. She thinks of it as a "Treasure Hunt" and has found many useful items for a good price.

One day, she observed a man carrying a large box out of a garage. She stopped the car and approached the man carrying the box. Out of the corner of her eye she saw a television set and asked the man how much he was asking for the TV? He told her it was not for sale and walked on. She looked at the man and with a knowing grin she said, "Ha-Ha" and walked on into the garage. The man followed her in and finally managed to convince her that he was really moving and the garage sale was on down the street.

Dr. J. Terry Hall

I was sharing stories with a group of kindergarten students at Abraham's birthplace in Lodgenville, Kentucky. I have a close friend who looks exactly like Abraham Lincoln down to the mole on his cheek and the way he wears his hair. He assumes the role of Lincoln and visits many schools, organizations and agencies in Kentucky. This day, my friend came over to say hello. Well, I was in the middle of a story about Lincoln's boyhood, so he waited to say hello. After I finished my story he walked over to where I was sitting. One of the kindergarten children was talking with one of his classmates. He took one look at my friend and said, 'Hey, she was just telling stories about you. Everyone thinks you are dead. Where have you been all of these years?'

Dr. Judy Pierce

The first year I taught school, I saved enough money to buy a used horse. He was a beautiful horse in my eyes. But after riding him for a short time, I realized that he had trouble walking. The owner of the stable, Mr. Sunday, where I boarded him, found a farmer who wanted to buy him for his children. So, I let him go to this nice farm. Mr. Sunday said he had a horse that I could buy. It was a beautiful palomino named Starlight, Starlight and I got along fine except he was so fat. It would be difficult to show him in a pleasure class at a horse show. He wanted to sale the horse, but couldn't find anyone who would buy the gelding.

My friend and I decided we would enter the costume class at the next show. He would be a Sheik and I would be a harm girl. One of the mothers in my school was a seamstress. We met and decided on the color of the outfit that I would wear in the costume class. She made me the most beautiful blue outfit trimmed in gold including the head gear that would cover my face. There was a matching saddle pad for the gilding I was to ride. I even covered the halter in blue and had a blue lead rope. Everything was ready for the first time we were to show in the costume class. At the show Brad was on his mare and was leading my horse as was done in Arabia at that time. We were doing well, that is, until a stallion behind me got a good whiff of Brad's mare who was open to be in heat. He had no idea that the mare was in season. Well, what can I say! That stallion threw his rider and passed me up as he was bent on getting close to that mare. Brad was so startled that he dropped the lead rope and left me hanging. He was trying to see what was happening. I had no rains and could not hold on to the saddle horn; so I held on to the horses' mane. The stallion confused my horse, who wanted to run to get out of the way of the stallion. The stallion was trying to mount Brad's mare with him on her. So, for about five minutes Brad was holding on for dear life. He was going up and down in the saddle while the mare reared and kept bucking. Brad could not dismount from the mare because of his costume. Apparently, she did not want any part of the stallion. But that stallion was not going to take no for an answer. Meanwhile, the owner of the stallion rushed into the ring trying his best to get the stallion away from the mare. He could not handle the stallion by himself, so two other men rushed into the ring. Finally, they got the stallion under control. The audience was laughing so hard; they couldn't stop if they had wanted to. Well, I can tell you, after that episode, we did not show in anymore costume classes.

Dr. Judy Pierce

Chapter 10

When I turned nine-years-old, I still believed in Santa. Several of the boys at school would laugh and make fun of me for still believing Santa was real. Finally, one day, I had enough of their making fun of me, so in a loud voice I shouted, "I know there is a Santa because my parents are poor and if there was not a Santa, I wouldn't get any presents". Later that year, I learned a lot. Now, with six grandchildren to buy presents for, I really wish there was a Santa.

Dr. J. Terry Hall

My Grand daddy told me this story. He said, "I was a farmer and some folks said I could grow fruit and vegetables on a rock, but I was especially proud of my prize watermelons. I would have watermelons larger than any of my neighbors. One year, just as my watermelons were becoming ripe, I noticed that some of my best watermelons were missing. I had a good idea who was stealing my melons, but I didn't want to confront the boys and make their parents mad. So, I came up with what I thought was a pretty good idea. I made me a sign and placed it in the middle of my watermelon patch. It read, "One of these watermelons is poisoned. Steal at your own risk!" For a few nights nothing was missing, so I figured the trick had worked. The following morning I went out to check on my melons to find printed on the sign. "Two of these watermelons are poisoned, eat at your own risk!" I had to let that crop of watermelons rot in the field.

Dr. J. Terry Hall

My son Ben, was a member of the Junior Chamber of Commerce and always attended the yearly banquet held somewhere in North Carolina. They always had a prize for the person who came dressed in the best costume One year, Ben cut out a big round cardboard circle, cut a hole in the center, and placed a light shade on his head. He received a lot of attention from people trying to figure out what his costume represented. When he told what his costume represented, he said, "I'm a one night stand." He won the prize

Ben F. Hall

My mother, Elizabeth Hall told me this story. The story goes to show even in a horrible situation, there is always some humor to be found. Although, Tompkinsville, Kentucky was in south central Kentucky, there were few tornadoes that took place in the area. The largest and most deadliest tornado took place in 1934. My mother was sixteen-years-old at the time and still lived with her parents. She and my daddy married when they were both eighteen. The tornado of 1934 killed many, many people in and around Tompkinsville. There was no plan for anything as horrible as this storm. Dead bodies were found everywhere. Broom straws were found stuck into trees and a 2x4 was found stuck in the motor block of a car. Also, an infant was found alive, but hanging up in a tree without a mark on him.

Even in disaster humor can shine through somehow. There was a town drunk who lived in Tompkinsville who we will call "Old Jack." "Old Jack" was usually found lying on the street and people would be so used to him that they would just step around him and go along with their business. When "Old Jack" was not passed, out he usually was smoking on a cigar. Well, the town people had decided to collect the dead and take them to the church house and lay them on a pew. You guessed it. They found "Old Jack" passed out and hoped he had slept through the storm and felt no pain. A black man who had been appointed to stay at the church and tell the people where to place the dead, pointed to a pew and "Old Jack" was placed on a pew. In a short time, the man looked back and observed smoke coming from "Old Jack's" body. All of a sudden, "Old Jack" pulled off the sheet and sat up, still smoking his cigar. The black man fell over in a dead faint.

Dr. J. Terry Hall

In 1970 we were fed up with the U.S. and decided to take a trip to Canada, with thoughts of moving there. We traveled from Indianapolis, up through Detroit and ended up in Owen Sound, a town at the south end of Georgian Bay. The town is in a bowl-like valley that everyone says just fills up with snow.

One night, my wife woke me up and said she thought the hotel was on fire. We were on the top third floor. I checked the door and when I didn't feel heat, I opened it to see billowing smoke emitting from an end stairway; Turned out it was a smoky mattress fire.

The next evening we heard about an upcoming blizzard due tomorrow. Early the next morning, it was already snowing. So I put some tire grips on our car and we headed due south, hoping to beat the lake effect blizzard. About twenty miles south, there was no snow so I took off the now noisy tire grips. As we headed further, it started to snow again. At first just flurries, but the further we went, the worse it got. By now we were afraid to stop, as visibility was near zero. There was a state truck in front of us. All I could see was his tail lights and an occasional light pole. Linda had the radio on, and I heard them say all roads to Mount Forest were now closed. I asked her what town we were headed for, as I wanted to stop. You guessed it, it was Mount Forest. The snow lightened up. My wife convinced me to keep going. When I got to the top of the hill, visibility was again zero. I thought I was just driving in fallen snow, but whump! I plowed right into a snow drift. The snow was over the hood. We got out to walk to town, but when I opened the driver's side door, I looked down to see the center line. We didn't go off the road, it was just a huge drift. As we walked down the hill, we met a snow plow. I warned him that my car was in the middle of the road, and hoped he wouldn't just push it aside. We walked down the hill and got a room at an old two story wooden hotel for eight dollars. In talking with locals, a guy convinced me we should get our car moved, so we walked back up to the car. I don't know how he did it, with our rear wheel drive car, but he got it out of the drift and into the parking lot.

The next morning, from our second floor room, we woke up to noises outside our room. They were shoveling snow off the roof! I checked the car and in front of the radiator was a huge block of ice, so I chipped out a small area so air could get through and hoped the engine wouldn't overheat. We heard the road was blocked by a stuck bus and truck. A bus driver said "he would try to make it through, and if he didn't come back in two hours, we'd know it is safe for us to head south again." It took him three tries and was 3 p.m. before we could leave. The car ran fine, but some parts of the road were plowed only for one lane. We finally made it to Kitchener, just twenty-miles south of Mount Forest, where they had about three inches of snow. Needless to say, we were happy to get back to Indy and decided that maybe the good old U.S.A. wasn't so bad after all.

Steve Jones

Class started for the first day of kindergarten. The kindergarten teacher said, "Hello class, my name is Ms. Smith." Wanting to start off on the right foot by talking about something they would be interested in, she continued, "How many of you are Philadelphia Eagles fans?" Everyone in class raised their hands except one little boy. Ms. Smith turned to the child and said, "And what is your name?" He replied, "I am Johnny." She asked. "And why are you not an Eagles fan, Johnny?" Johnny replied, "I am a Dallas Cowboys fan." Mrs. Smith asked why and he said, "My mom and dad are Cowboys fans." Ms. Smith said, well if your dad and mom were idiots would that make you an idiot also? "No Ma'am, that would make me an Eagles fan."

Ben F. Hall

When I was acting as Assistant Principal at Warren Elementary School in Bowling Green, Kentucky, I had this one Teacher Assistant who was always complaining about things other teachers had done and how it had hurt her feelings. One day she stomped into my office and said in a loud voice, "I need to talk to you, I've got a problem! I had it up to here with her and her "problems." So I said, "Is it a big problem or a small problem?" She shouted, "It's a BIG problem!" I pushed my chair back and replied, then you need to go next door to the Principal's office, I only handle small problems."

Dr. J. Terry Hall

Chapter 11

I worked with the State Department of Education as a program coordinator for reading and social studies for two years. There were other coordinators for art, science, foreign language, music and math. During that time, we traveled the state together training teachers and administrators regarding the new policies on education. We would load up a state van with all the materials that we would need for each trip. Generally, Mr. Long, our boss, would ride in the van with the driver. The rest of us car pooled. Many times we would be gone for an entire week and sometimes weekends.

It was about 1 a.m. one Saturday morning when the coordinator for science, Mr. Winfield, Mr. Long, Mr. Cool and I were returning to the capital city after being gone for the entire week. As usually, Mr. Winfield was driving the van and Mr. Cook was the passenger. We were about twenty-five miles from home on a two lane road way up in the mountains that some people say, had as many curves as Mae West. I believe whoever came up with that analogy was correct.

The coordinator of foreign languages, Mr. Cook and I were riding together and following close behind the van. It was so foggy we could barely see the tail lights of the van. Suddenly, the van stopped in a curve in the middle of the road. I thought it odd that they did not flash their emergency lights. Of course, Mr. Cook, stopped behind the van and put on the emergence lights on the car. I asked, "I wonder what is going on? Maybe one of us should get out of the car and walk up to the van and find out what is happening." Mr. Cook was concerned about getting out of the car due to the fog and said, "They have stopped for a good reason. Lets just wait this out. We could not imagine what the problem was with the van. I said, maybe someone is ill. Mr. Cook said, "That is not likely. Let's just wait."

Wait is just what we did! Hours passed and we didn't move. No one came from the opposite direction. After all, who in their right mind would be on that highway at 1:00 a.m. Finally, about 3:00a.m., the van started moving forward with us following close behind. Once we got to the capital city and unloaded the van, Mr. Cook and I were informed that the van had to stop for a huge, black mother bear and her cubs sitting in the middle of the road.

Dr. Judy Pierce

After the first year of teaching, a friend, Donna and I decided to travel to Lexington, Kentucky to visit some of the thoroughbred horse farms. Instead of driving to Lexington in my Corvair, we decided to travel on a Greyhound bus. We did not travel in my car because the fan belt would come off when it wanted to and the drive to Lexington was a long one.

Donna and I arrived in Lexington early one afternoon. I rented a luxury car because that was the only one available. The day was absolutely beautiful with the sun shining brightly. We drove to all the horse farms who were open to the public and just had a great time. That evening Donna and I decided that we would like to see a movie. We got to the theater and I parked the car on the street. After the movie ended, it was dark as we walked to the car. I put the key in the door lock, but it would not open. I tried the key several times on both sides, and to no avail. Suddenly, Donna burst out laughing. I said, "What is so funny? Looks like we are going to have to walk back to the motel." She said, "Look at the car next to this one." I asked, "Why?" She said, "Just look." I did, and wow! There was the same car, the same color parked right next to our rental car. Only, that was not our rental car. It seems I was trying to unlock a car that was owned by another person. I laughed until my sides hurt. Well, we made it back to the motel and home.

Dr. Judy Pierce

I love living in North Carolina, but Kentucky will always be close to my heart. It is where I took my first steps and where many memories were made. I am not going to say it is where I grew up, because I don't think, even now, that I have grown up. As long as there is breath in my body and my mind is somewhat normal, I am still growing up with every day the Good Lord allows me to stay around.

Coming from a cattle farm background, I loved working with registered Black Angus Cattle. Many times after I had moved to Asheville, North Carolina, I would travel back to Tompkinsville to visit with family and friends. During those times, I would go out in the field where the cattle grazed, walk to a large oak tree in the middle of the pasture, and just watch the cattle move peacefully around me.

I guess this feeling is the reason this sign caused me to chuckle. One day, I was driving up Interstate 65 just north of Bowling Green, Kentucky when I saw a big sign along the road which read; USED COWS FOR SALE!

Dr. J. Terry Hall

Another thing I enjoy is flying. Taking a flight across the country in a window seat is very enjoyable. I even took several flight lessons while I lived in Glasgow, Kentucky.

When I began my flight training, in a Piper Cub, I was told that it would take me about fourteen hours of instructor training before I would be able to solo. That sounded good to me, so I climbed in and we took off doing what was called touch and go. I would take off, fly around the airport and come in for a landing.

One Saturday, I went over for my instructor training and the instructor let me fly around the airport and land. This time, when I pulled in on the tarmac and switched off the engine, the instructor said, "Don't unbuckle. You are going to solo." I swallowed, and told him I had only seven hours instructor time. He said, "I'm aware of that, and if I didn't know you could do it I would not allow you to solo in my plane." I took a deep breath and said, "OK."

I taxied out to the end of the runway, throttled in and the plane started going down the runway. Just as soon as the airplane lifted off the ground I glanced over to the right seat at where the instructor was sitting only moments before. It hit me like a ton of bricks, "It was totally up to me to land this thing." I flew around the pattern as it was called and came in for a perfect three point landing.

As soon as the plane had touched the ground, my right leg began to jerk uncontrollable due to a muscle cramp because of the stress placed on it while flying. I reached down with my right arm and gripped the jerking leg with all my might. The only thing that that accomplished was to make my whole body shake. I managed to bring it on in on the tarmac and shut off the engine. I unbuckled and climbed out of the plane. When my feet hit the ground, they would not hold me up and I had to grab hold of the struts to keep from falling. The instructor came over with a pair of scissors and cut off my shirttail as was the custom after a solo flight, and placed it on the bulletin board with my name and date of my solo flight.

Dr. J. Terry Hall

Chapter 12

I received my Emergency Medical Technology, (EMT) certification and volunteered with the Asheville Area Rescue Squad where I served for six years. During that time, I became friends with several other volunteers, one being Larry Robinson. Larry told me a couple of stories that although tragic, had some humor. If an EMT cannot see some humor in the job, they need to move on before they have a mental breakdown. This is Larry's story: One night around midnight my tones sounded and reported a fight with injuries at a local bar down below the VA hospital. Arriving on the scene, I found a big man, probably well over three hundred pounds, lying on the ground bleeding profusely from the back of his head. The man was drunk and cussing up a storm. He was yelling at the top of his voice about this "Slut" and how he was going to kill her.

As we administered direct pressure to his head to control the bleeding, while kneeling down on one knee, we heard a woman scream directly above our head, "You ###of a ### if you don't shut your trap, I'll finish the job!" Looking up we observed a little woman, most likely weighing less than a hundred pounds soaking wet, standing over us shaking a pool stick.

My guess was that the woman had said, "Shut up!" and the man thought she had said, "Stand up!" He will most likely listen better next time.

Larry Robinson

When I was growing up in West Virginia, my sister and I had many playgrounds that children dream about: There was a creek with a pier and a red john boat attached, a main highway, railroad track where we could pick up pieces of coal, a quarry for any kind of rocks that could be collected, and a swamp a short distance up the road. In the swamp, there were cattails, green snakes, and other critters that children might like to collect.

Every summer, I would go fishing in the creek and collect catfish and sometimes turtles. The fish and turtles could not be eaten due to poison run-offs from a plant up the river. So I would just throw them back in the creek. I continued to love fishing throughout my life, but there was a point where I stopped fishing for many years.

About five years ago, a friend and his wife from North Carolina came to Kentucky to visit and asked if I would like to come over to their campsite and go fishing. I had a new fishing rod and was very excited at the prospect. Well, it had been many years since I had put a fishing worm on the hook and that slippery little creature just would not stay on the hook. So, my friend baited my hook. I swung back my fishing pole to put the line in the water. Unfortunately, I did not hit the water, but the back of a chair. Later that week, my neighbor asked if I caught anything. I said, "Yes, sure did. I caught the biggest thing I ever caught fishing; the back of a chair."

Dr. Judy Pierce

My mother and her sister lived in Florida for about seventeen years. During that time, Mother said that, "She would like to have a coal flower." Since there was no coal in Florida, she asked if I could get her a piece in West Virginia. I told her that I would get her a piece of coal and make her a coal flower.

I purchased a large piece of coal and a big fish bowl to hold it. It took a while to find the mercurochrome and bluing as they were items that were no longer available in supermarkets and drug stores. After getting the ingredients and putting them together, I placed the project in the dark for two weeks. After that period of time, I removed the coal from the darkness and it was beautiful. I told Mother I would mail it to her in Florida. So I wrapped the coal flower in the fish bowl carefully and packed it in a box so it would not get broken.

Well, it arrived safely and Mother just loved it so much that she kept it in the living room on her coffee table. I told her to keep adding a little salt to it each day so it would grow more.

Later that year, my family decided to come home to West Virginia for a short visit. Mother asked a neighbor to water the indoor plants and to take special care of her coal flower. Her neighbor happily agreed to do so the week that the family was gone. After my family returned to Florida, mother was anxious to see how much the coal flower had grown. When she looked at the fish bowl containing the flower, it was full of water. Her neighbor thought the coal flower was an indoor plant and watered it each day. Mother had a fit! She called and said, "My coal flower is gone because my neighbor watered it every day." I asked, "Do you want another one?" She said, "No, I'm someone else might mistake the coal flower for a real plant."

Dr. Judy Pierce

A friend and I taught in Winston Salem, N.C. for many years. We taught in different inner-city schools and different grade levels. Sally Mae taught sixth grade while I taught fifth grade. Our teaching methods in social studies were about the same even though the content was different. Sally Mae focused more on world history such as Italy, Germany, Mexico, China, Latin American and so on. I focused more on U.S. History, from its famous explorers like Cortez and Sir Walter Raleigh to Reconstruction after the Civil War. Each of us would bring artifacts into the classroom to enhance whatever topic in social studies that was being addressed. This really helped the inner-city children without having a background knowledge of the topic. They could see, taste, and feel those artifacts.

Well, Sally Mae told me that her class was going to study Germany and what artifacts she was going to bring to class. It really sounded great and would really excite her students.

One day during the study of Germany, she noticed that the class was very quiet during lunch; this was most unusual for the boys and girls. Sally Mae knew that something was going on, but could not put a finger on it.

Well, after lunch, the students were given the opportunity to go to the restroom and to get a drink of water. One of the students came up to Sally Mae and said, "Mrs. Wilkins, Shakia brought a can of beer to school today and we were all sipping it during lunch." Sally Mae could not believe her ears. Her first thoughts were: "I am going to get fired because this school is next door to a church." Well, when Shakia was ready to come into the classroom, Sally Mae said, "What did you bring to lunch today Shakia? What did you drink?" Shakia said, "Mrs. Wilkins I brought a can of soda pop to drink with my lunch," Sally Mae said, "Now you know that the school does not allow students to bring drinks like that to school. Go to the cafeteria and get the can out of the garbage before you get in trouble." "But Mrs. Wilkins, do I have to go get the can?" Shakia was dancing around like she had bees in her pants. Sally Mae said, "Yes, you do. Now go and get the can." Saakia said, "But Mrs. Wilkins I can't get the can." Sally Mae said, "Why Shakia?" Shakia said, "Oh, Mrs. Wilkins, I got into my daddy's beer and brought a can to school today. We have been studying German yand beer is one of the country's main products. I just thought the class would enjoy a can." Well, the school year ended and no one found out what the students had done.

Dr. Judy Pierce

I grew up on a tobacco farm in south central Kentucky. Tobacco was a year round conversation. In the winter they talked about how many acres they were going to set in tobacco; in the spring, they talked about getting the tobacco bed sowed; in the summer, it was about suckering the tobacco; and in the fall, it was about stripping the tobacco and taking it to market. Well, one can see that tobacco was a very important part of our lives

My grandfather, Cecil B. Hall, everybody called him CB, was a very important part of this cycle. CB was the type of person who had to show you how things were done. He never just told about how something or the other was done, he had to show you.

One year we had finished cutting tobacco and was in the process of hanging it in the barn to dry. Kentucky tobacco was always allowed time to air dry in a tobac co barn. This year CB had gone over to the barn early to hang some tobacco, which were on tobacco sticks and were hung high in the tobacco barn. He stood up on one of the high tiers where he was to hang the tobacco stick and when he raised up he hit his head on the tier and nearly knocked himself out.

A short time later, CB's two sons, Frank and Leroy came over to help their father. As soon as they arrived, CB began telling them about hitting his head. As he continued telling his story, he raised his head quickly, hit his head and fell off the tier. He never did live that one down.

Dr. J. Terry Hall

Chapter 13

My grandson, Bo, who is six years old, was listening to his mom and dad discuss the subject of dating with an older brother. Mom looked at Bo and said," Before long, you will meet some pretty girl, fall in love with her and love each other like your dad and I do." Bo, looked up at her and making a face said, "That is gross!"

Ben F. Hall

Not long after Patricia and I married, she made sure that I would get the point. I have always had a problem with weight. I tried everything in the book to lose weight, but to no avail. One day, I saw an advertisement about a medication that guaranteed weight loss. I needed a prescription in order to try it and made a doctor's appointment. I was informed that he would prescribe the medication, but it needed to be given by an injection. Well, I have always been afraid of needles and this bothered be, but I said, "OK, I will try it."

That night I told Patricia that I just could not give myself the injection and asked her to give me the shot. I dropped my pants and asked her to give it in the hip. Well, she did not tell me that she was terrified about giving me the injection. We were standing in the bathroom in front of a mirror and she jabbed me in the butt. Just as soon as the needle went in, she screamed and ran across the bathroom. I quickly, looked at the mirror to see the needle dangling in my butt, I yelled, "PUSH IT IN! PUSH IT IN!" She finally calmed down enough until she could push the needle in and then screamed again.

Dr. J. Terry Hall

Another story, was after I had received my Doctor of Education Degree and was working as an Elementary School Supervisor and Title 1 Director for Asheville City schools. I had a wonderful secretary who was always there to work with me and knew the programs well. I give her credit in working with me all those years and teaching me the job.

One day, I was very busy working on our year-end report. All of a sudden, I looked all over my desk for my glasses, but to no avail. Finally, I walked over to Roberta's desk and asked, "Roberta, have you seen my glasses? I have looked everywhere and they can not be found?" Roberta looked up and laughed. She said, "They are on your head." I am sure, under her breath, she placed the word stupid at the beginning of the sentence.

Dr. J. Terry Hall

No one has ever accused me of being directionally sound. I can turn around twice and I am confused as to which way to go. A story to prove the point happened just a few days ago. My grandson, lives in our downstairs apartment and uses the back of the basement to do his workouts with a barbell. The back of the basement has a light on a pull cord just inside the door and a switch on the other side of the room.

One night, I entered the back basement and instead of pulling the pull cord, I felt I knew the way across the room to the light switch. As I crossed the dark room, I became disorientated and could not tell which way to go. I felt the wall and continued feeling for the light switch. All of a sudden, I tripped over the barbell and fell. I had hurt my leg and still didn't know which way to go. I reached for my cell phone to call my wife, Patricia, then I realized I had left it upstairs. I managed to crawl around on the floor until I finally found the light switch. I never thought I would get lost in my own basement.

Dr. J. Terry Hall

A close friend of mine has a daughter who was and is, one the most intelligent people I know anywhere. She is almost grown at the time, but this story goes back a few years when she was a young child. One day she walked in the bathroom and observed her father standing and urinating in the commode. Startled, the father said, "Go back in the bedroom; I will be out in a minute." She turned to leave and as she made her way out the door, she stopped and he heard her say, "How did he do that?"

Dr. J. Terry Hall

My sister, mother and I used to love to go to gospel concerts with some very well known singers. One day, Mother told her sister that her hair was getting long and that she needed a permanent. My aunt did a good job cutting hair and giving perms even though she was not professionally trained. Shortly, thereafter, my sister and her boyfriend, mother and I decided to go to a gospel concert. Well, mother couldn't go with her hair the way it looked. So on the day of the concert, my aunt cut her hair and gave her a permanent.

When we left the house, Mother wore a head scarf, which was nothing unusual.

As we sat down in front of the stage, the lights were dimmer and the lights on the stage became very bright. I was sitting beside mother when I noticed something unusual about her hair. I looked closely and noticed that her hair was not the beautiful brown color, but aqua. Apparently, something went wrong when my aunt was giving her the permanent. I touched my sister and said, "Look at Mother's hair." We got tickled.

Well, I can tell you the next day, Mother's hair was no longer aqua. She dyed her hair with some brown color that looked worse than the aqua color. She told my aunt, "I don't think you will ever give me another perm." In a few weeks, mother's hair had grown out enough that she could finally cut off all the ugly brown color. From that time on, my aunt never gave Mother another permanent.

Dr. Judy Pierce

I taught fifth grade in an inner-city school in Winston Salem, North Carolina. The school principal, Mr. Williams required the faculty to stand by their classroom door the first day the students came to school and every day thereafter. It was the first day of my last year teaching at this school. I was standing in the doorway of my classroom, waiting for my last student to arrive. Low and behold, here came my last student walking down the hallway. He was a really cute student. He walked up to me and asked, "Are you Fierce Pierce?" I said, "Yes, and what's your name?"

Dr. Judy Pierce

Several years ago when my grandson, Dakota was about four, my wife and I were living in Bowling Green, Kentucky where I was serving as Assistant Principal while taking care of my parents in their later years. My son and his wife brought Dakota to Bowling Green to spend a week with us.

One bright sunny day I took Dakota outside to fly a kite that I had given him. All was going great, just a grandson and his granddad enjoying being together. As I was running full speed, with the kite up in the air, everything was wonderful until I approached a deep ditch that had been dug to slow the water down. They had placed big boulders along the bottom of the ditch to keep it from washing. Well, you guess it. I ran right into that ditch at full speed and crashed into the boulders. I was bleeding from my head and had cuts and scrapes in my arms and legs.

Dakota ran on into the apartment with tears in his eyes. Patricia asked him what was the matter, he said, "I'm mad!" She asked, "Why are you mad?" He said, "Pap-Paw got my kite caught in a tree!" She said, "Where is Pap-Paw?" Dakota looked up through his tears and said, "He is lying out there in the ditch."

Dakota Hall

My parents married in 1934 in the small town of Tompkinsville, Kentucky. They were both eighteen years old and, even though it was in the middle of the Great Depression, they could think of nothing other than spending their lives together.

The newlyweds, had no choice but to find a place to rent. They rented a bedroom and bath with a shared kitchen from an old woman who had never married and was dedicated to her church.

One Saturday morning the newlyweds were enjoying each other like newly weds do. There was a lot of giggling, and noises, when they heard a loud banging on the bedroom wall and the old woman yelled, "You two would be better off studying your Sunday School lesson".

Dr. J. Terry Hall

I was a lifeguard at Fort Bragg Officer's Mess. There were two pools; one for families one for adults. Periodically, we would close one of the pools to clean any algae and fungi buildup. To do this, we would add chemicals and turn up the chlorine to high levels. This of course, made it unsafe for swimming. Overnight, the chemicals would turn off and the pool would be ready for swimming the next morning.

I was on the guard stand and heard a splash in the pool that was clearly marked closed. I walked over and a man was doing laps. I said, "Excuse me, Sir, but this pool is closed for the day. He replied, "I am General so and so and I will swim anywhere I GD please!" I replied, "Yes Sir," I wanted to just let him swim in those chemicals, but thought I should do the right thing. I went over to the woman and asked her if she was his wife. She indicated she was. I told her we turned up the chlorine and added very harsh chemicals to kill the algae and it was unsafe to swim there. I also told her I didn't know what it would do to his eyes and she may want to get him checked out when he finished his swim. I returned to my stand and within minutes, I heard a loud profanity from the other pool and the gate slam. I wondered if there would be repercussions, but there were none.

Donald Carter

My father, a Colonel in the Army Special Forces, was always playing tricks and jokes on people.

Being an avid golfer, my father told me about a time he was out playing golf with a friend. After his friend hit a drive that he was proud of, my father said, "I bet you five dollars I can throw a golf ball further than you can hit it with a golf club." Needless to say, his friend was more than ready to take that bet. "I'll need a little time to warm up my arm. I'll let you know when I'm ready." The next time they had to make a parachute jump, my father stood in the doorway of the airplane, held a golf ball, looked over and said, "Hey Frank, I'm ready," then threw the golf ball out the door. Frank said, "You SOB," and handed him the five dollars.

Donald Carter

After my father retired, his granddaughter joined the army. She finished her basic training and was assigned to her new posting. In order to give her a little help, he called several Generals he had worked for during his career and asked them to write a letter and give her some encouragement in her career in the army. It wasn't too long before the Base Commander came over and asked her how she was doing. She started to receive letter after letter from active and retired generals in the army. My father called her and asked about how things were going for her. She said, "Great, these are the nicest people you would ever want to meet. Everybody was so nice and helpful."

Donald Carter

My father's good friend was a Mexican-American named Al. They served for years in the military together. My dad said, "Al, tell Don how your brother was killed." My father got great amusement about asking Al, to tell people how his brother was killed. Needless to say, I was confused how this could be humorous until I heard Al tell the story with his Spanish accent. "One day my brother get drunk and fell asleep on the railroad track. The train was coming and he didn't hear the weasel." My father would snicker. Al said, "I don't know why he finds that funny?"

Donald Carter

Chapter 14

My grandfather Frank moved to Hobbs, New Mexico in the early part of the twentieth century. He was hired to clean out a Well. Here is the story:

There is a place called Monument, named after a large stack of rocks the Apache and Comanche placed there to help them locate the well because the prairie was very flat with scrub grass and went on forever. In order to locate the well when they were crossing, they built a small mountain of stones that they could see from a long way

When the ranchers came and settled that area, they wouldn't let the Native Americans back in to get the water.

One night, the Indians slipped in and took all the stones and threw them into the well to block it off. It worked. Years later, the town of Hobbs hired my grandfather to clean the well out and get the water flowing again. With a crew of men, he did get the stones out of the well, but the water did not flow. They then hired him to place several pumps around the well. That worked and they are still using that water today.

Donald Carter

I was on my way to the International Reading Conference. I sat beside an Irish couple, and the woman asked me where I was going. I told her to an IRA Conference. They looked at each other and were very quiet for awhile. Then she spoke up and said, "They have a Conference?" In a moment, I put it all together and said, "International Reading Association." They gave a sigh of relief and said, "Oh."

Donald Carter

An ancestor of mine in the eighteen hundreds owned a farm in Robeson County, North Carolina. The house (3-4) rooms was built at an earlier time in the middle of the property on a hill. My ancestor had two sons and several daughters. Upon his death, he left the property to be divided between his sons. The two sons argued and squabbled continuously on who was entitled to the house (as it stood in the center of the property.) They were both very angry and neither one was willing to compromise on what was to be done about the house. The older son left the farm to handle some business in Lumberton, the county seat and was gone for two or three days. Upon his return, with his wagon and mules, imagine his astonishment upon finding the house had been sawed in half. Family lore states they came to some solution, but never spoke to each other ever again. I love my family!

Beth Bulluck Carter

The ladies in my family have a celebration "Rite of Passage" when one matures from a young girl to a lady. We celebrate by having a party, sharing stories of our times and giving gifts and advise to the young lady becoming a woman. Upon my granddaughter's initiation into "Ladies' Club," she was very excited and, after giving details of her initiation she said, "Thank God that is over with!" We all went very quiet and didn't know what to say. It appears she thought this was a one-time thing. Sadly, we had to let her know this was a monthly experience.

Beth Bulluck Carter

My grandparents were born in Robeson County, North Carolina, but my grandfather could not inherit the farm as he was a younger son. He moved his family to Rocky Mount, North Carolina in the 1920s to work with the railroad. Each summer my grandmother would send William, the older son, to my grandfather's family and Ashley the younger son, to her family (since they traveled free as grandfather was a railroad employee.)

One year, as William was on the return trip to Rocky Mount, the train did not stop for his brother, Ashley. William was very concerned and asked a porter about his brother. The porter told William that Ashley went home earlier that month. The porter further told him that one or two of his uncles had a moonshine still on one of the aits (a river island) and several boys including Ashley, (Ashley did not know what a moonshine still was) had discovered it. The uncles weren't too concerned about revenuers, but they were terrified that their sister would find out and what she would say to them as she was a born again Christian.

Beth Bulluck Carter

Great aunt Annie, a primitive Baptist had passed away. Our family of three young children and one young cousin were attending the funeral. My father was a pall bearer, escorted my mother, aunt, siblings, cousin and myself into the church. We were Baptist and unaware of the Primitive Baptist ceremonies and rites. We had pianos and organs in our ceremonies, but the Primitive Baptist having no musical instruments and chanted their songs.

Once the ceremony started without musical instruments, we were startled and we four children started giggling. Aunt Earl and

Mama glared at us to hush up but, then, they got tickled too. How inappropriate! My father was told to immediately escort us out of the church, then returned to do his job as pall bearer. My mother and aunt said they could never attend family reunions after this episode and we never did.

Beth Bulluck Carter

My friend, William moved from Yellowstone National Park to a famous historic site, in Kentucky. William's basic job was to train interpreters for the historical site and sometimes, be a tour guide. Not long ago, the organization that operates the historical site decided to restore the exterior of two of the buildings. This one day, William was guiding a tour and sharing with them the history of the area. He mentioned that all the buildings were over two hundred years old. One of the middle aged men in the group said, "Well, it looks like from those scaffolds that you are building some new buildings.

Dr. Judy Pierce

One day my son Ben was frying chicken and talking to his stepson, Robby Foster. Robby asked Ben, "What are you doing?" Ben said,

"Frying chicken." Robby looked confused as he said, "I thought chicken came from a box." (meaning KFC) Robby is not a farm boy.

Robby Foster

Say what! A road near my house is named Future Road. Right next to the road sign was a sign that said, Dead end! I am glad I do not live there.

Dr. J. Terry Hall

My grandmother, Bassie Jane, got a new telephone in the 1950s. At that time there was not many private lines and when you received a call it would ring once, twice or three rings. That way you would know if the call was for you or for someone else on your party line. The problem was if the call was not for you, but someone else on the party line, there was always the temptation to quietly pick up the receiver and listen in on their conservation.

One day the phone rang twice and everyone knew it was for my grandmother. She answered and the conversation soon turned to gossip from the neighborhood. Now Alice was as bad, if not worst as anyone to listen in on the "private" conservation. My grandmother had just told something about someone down the road getting into trouble when

Alice broke in and said, "That ain't the truth. I know that woman and she ain't no hussy!"

A few months later, I suggested to my grandmother that she should get a private line. She had a fit and said, "That's crazy! How in the world would I know what was going on in the community?"

Dr. J. Terry Hall

Shortly after Patricia and I married, we rented an apartment across the street from where we were going to college in Nashville, Tennessee. One afternoon I came in from class and Patricia suggested we drive down to Memphis, Tennessee, around two hundred miles so she could cash in some "Green Stamps." Green Stamps were given at stores and could be cashed in at certain locations for items. Why we had to travel so far I still do not understand.

Well, we traveled to the outskirts of Memphis and it was getting dark. We decided to find a room to spend the night. The trouble was that we only had twenty dollars between us for a room. We finally found a rooming house and went in to inquire about a room. We first told the woman we only had twenty dollars and asked if we could stay for that amount. She agreed and took us to a room. Everything looked OK except there were cat hairs all over the bed. We decided that the last people who rented the room had most likely had a cat. We were tired and went right to bed.

During the night, we heard an awful noise and woke up to see a wharf rat the size of a big cat strolled slowly across the floor. We grabbed one another and hugged all night long. We never closed our eyes through the night for fear that we would be eaten by the rat. Half asleep we made it to the Green Stamp store and then back to our safe apartment in Nashville.

Dr. J. Terry Hall

Back in the day, most folks did not even lock their doors when they went to bed, much less their car doors. Patricia and I had just purchased our first car, a brand new black 1966 Mustang for $2000. and were making monthly payments on it. One day, after work, we decided to go to K-Mart and just look around; we sure couldn't afford much of anything with our car payment of $60. and our rent of $65 per month.

Well, when we started home, we spotted our Mustang across the parking lot and went over and got in; I had trouble getting my key to work when Patricia spotted another Mustang two rows over. We went over to the car, laughing at our mistake. When I tried the key, you guessed it, the key did not start the car. Getting frustrated, we finally on the third try, found our car and made it home.

Dr. J. Terry Hall

One day I will never forget, was when I had finished my undergraduate work at David Lipscomb College and was scheduled for my graduation. My parents were coming down from Kentucky for my graduation and I was very excited.

About three hours before I was supposed to walk across the stage, and receive my diploma, I once again walked to the front door to see if I could see my parents coming in the driveway. Well, as I opened the screen door a wasp hit me right between the eyes. By the time I walked across the stage, I looked like an Oriental with both my eyes nearly closed. But I made it!

Dr. J. Terry Hall

Chapter 15

Patricia and I married in 1965 and moved into an apartment across from the college. I was limber and a little overweight. Patricia's parents came up from North Carolina for their first visit to our new home and I was proud to be their daughter's strong husband. I was taking my new father-in-law around the yard when I decided to reach up to a low hanging limb and pull myself up. I have asked myself why I did that for the past fifty-three years. Well, as you may have guessed, as I pulled myself upward and pulled both feet up on the tree, the limb broke and I landed butt first on the hard ground. So much for macho.

Dr. J. Terry Hall

My mother, Elizabeth related this story to me about her mother Kate. Living in the early 1900s, Kate and her husband, Frank lived in a small house along the side of the road. Every night they would raise the window at the head of their bed to let cool air into their bedroom. One night while they were sleeping soundly, they heard a terrible sound. It sounded like some giant monster was coming into their bedroom. Jumping up in panic they observed a mule with his head stuck through the window just above their heads.

It seemed that the local drunk had passed out while riding his mule and the mule had wandered over to their house and decided to look in their bedroom and bray.

Dr. J. Terry Hall

In 1998, Patricia and I were living in Bowling Green, Kentucky. We discovered that an older woman, Dona, lived in Bowling Green and attended church where we attended. Dona had grown up with my mother Elizabeth and we all became the best of friends.

Dona, had retired from "Fruit of the Loom" at sixty-five and had worked for the past thirty-five years rocking babies at the Western Kentucky University Nursery. She was still working there when she turned one hundred years old.

The local media made a big thing of this event and interviewed her on the local news. One of the questions they asked her was, "Do you have anyone who is an enemy?" Dona answered, "No I can truly say I have no enemies." The interviewer said, "It's hard to believe you have no enemy after one hundred years. How do you account for that?" Dona replied, "I outlived them all."

Dr. J. Terry Hall

While I was preaching at the Candler Church of Christ, an embarrassing thing happened to a member of the church. During services, she needed to go to the restroom. She quietly got up and made her way to restroom. After finishing, she made her way back to her pew with a long tail of toilet paper dragging behind her. It seems that the toilet paper got stuck in her panties as she pulled up her clothes. One of the kind ladies whispered to her and she hurried back to the restroom with a red face.

Dr. J. Terry Hall

As I finished up my Educational Leadership Degree at Western Carolina University, I was required to take an oral exam made up of four college administrators. I answered all the questions correctly except one. What is the required age for a child to start school? I had never had to deal with that issue and did not know if it was six or seven years old. The chairman of my committee told me to go research and come by his office when I had the answer. Five minutes later I walked into the professor's office and told him the required age was seven years old. He looked at me, then at his watch. He asked, "How did you do your research so quickly?" I quickly answered, "I called over to the Jackson County Board of Education and asked a secretary. He scratched his head as he said, "That is exactly what I would do. You will make an excellent administrator."

Dr. J. Terry Hall

One day, when Patricia and I were living in Kentucky, her parents were going back to Kentucky with us to stay a few days. This was before I-40 was completed and we had to cross the mountain between Cherokee, North Carolina and Tennessee.

As we were going down the mountain on the Tennessee side, we were stopped behind a line of traffic. Cars were lined up for over a mile. When we finally arrived at the end of the line of cars, we discovered a car stopped in the middle of the road, watching a black bear and her cubs on the side of the road. The mama bear had her front paws against the passenger's closed window where the man's wife, I suppose, was screaming. The man was sitting in the driver's seat with his window down and his left arm resting on the door. He was laughing his head off at the fit his wife was pitching. Ben Cochran was always up for a good laugh and as we slowly made our way around the stopped car, he reached his right arm out his window, slammed his hand hard several times and growled loudly like a bear. The man screamed and jumped over in his wife's lap.

Ben Cochran

While I was serving as Assistant Principal, I attended a conference at Pinehurst, North Carolina. Pinehurst is better known for it's golf course where many golf tournaments are held. I was just learning the game of golf at the time and when three women asked me if I would play a round of golf with them I was all for it. Well, the first hole was across a lake. Each of the women hit their balls half way to the green without any problem with the water. I teed up and hit my ball, very conscious of the three women watching. The ball went straight up and "Splash," into the water. I swallowed my pride and tried a second time. The ball followed the same course as the first, "Splash." I was very embarrassed and decided that was enough. So, I got another ball out of my bag, walked around the lake and teed up for the third time. Water was now out of the picture. I hit a long drive and as impossible as it sounds, the ball hit a small steel pipe in the middle of the fairway and bounced back into the water.

Dr. J. Terry Hall

A while back, my friend opened his computer to find a site for nudes. He had a seven-year-old girl and a fifteen-year-old boy. Of course, not blaming anyone, he looked at his son who just stared back and then he looked at his seven year old daughter and she said, "Don't look at me, I don't even have any boobs!"

Dr. J. Terry Hall

When I was around eleven-years-old, my cousin Jerry, who was about nine, visited the stock barn, where farmers brought their livestock to sell. Well, it didn't take very long for the two of us to become bored and begin to go throughout the barn to see what we could find.

It was a big barn and had a basement where stock was kept until the sale. There was no light in the basement and we were feeling our way through the hallway when all of a sudden something big slammed the gate and made a noise that sounded like it was going to eat us up. My cousin, Jerry broke into a full all out run while I stood there with my right leg bouncing up and down and my left leg froze to the ground. I have heard of people who were frozen stiff, but I was literally frozen stiff. It turned out to be a large boar hog that had charged the gate and tried to get at us.

Dr. J. Terry Hall

I don't remember where I heard this story but it begs to be retold: This family had two children, a fifteen-year-old boy and a six year old girl. It seems that a few weeks before, the boy had gotten hurt on the football field. He had taken a hit between the legs and it hurt something terrible. A few weeks later, the six year old girl fell off her scooter and bruised her knee. Her dad rushed to her and asked if she was hurt. She managed to get out between sobs, "I hurt my nuts!"

Dr. J. Terry Hall

I remember a Christmas Eve when Ben was about three years old. Patricia decided, after Ben had gone to sleep, to take flour and a pair of my shoes and placing the shoes in the flour she made foot prints up from the basement to the Christmas tree.

The next morning, when Ben awoke and came running from his bedroom to the Christmas tree to see what Santa had brought during the night.

Seeing the footprints he was sure that Santa was real.

Dr. J. Terry Hall

This story may make PETA angry, but I didn't do it my granddaddy did. My granddaddy, Cecil was a very hard-headed man when it came to working with his registered Black Angus cattle. I never knew a time when he did not get his way in forcing the cattle to do or go where he wanted them.

One time he was attempting to load a two-thousand-pound bull into a truck. He tried to get the stubborn bull to walk up the loading chute into a truck. The bull was determined he was not going up that chute and was pawing the ground and slinging dirt over his head. My granddaddy said, "Just go over there and rest, Terry, I will be back in a few minutes.

A few minutes later, he came back with an electric cord tied to a tobacco stick with two nails sticking out of the end of the stick. He then plugged in the cord and told me to step out of the way. He then walked around the bull and touched the bull on the hip. The bull threw back his head and looked at the chute. My granddaddy touched the two electric nails to the bull's balls. The bull snorted and ran full speed up the chute ramming his head against the cab of the truck. A little motivation goes a long way.

Dr. J. Terry Hall

One fond memory from my years teaching fifth grade students at Vance Elementary School in Asheville, North Carolina was one day I was teaching something or the other in social studies. And for some reason, it was one of those days when almost all the children were talking to each other, playing with their pencils or just sitting there like they were in another world.

All teachers could relate to days like this, but I was determined to get their attention. I kept on talking as I pulled out my desk chair, stepped up on the chair, and then stepped on up on my desk. You could have heard a pin drop as every child stopped talking and looked at me with their mouths open. After about a minute, I stepped down to the floor and never missed a word of my lesson. The rest of the time, I had no problem keeping their attention. I can imagine what they told their parents when they got home.

Dr. J. Terry Hall

Back in the day, and even today, people have sayings they would say when something unexpectedly happened, such as "My Goodness!" "Marcy Me!" or "Gracious!" Well, Lina Fortune had a saying which I had never heard. When she was surprised, she would say, "Well, I wish you would!" It was just a saying and she would say it and never realize what she had said.

Well, one day her saying got her in a heap of trouble. She had a boy in third grade who was always in trouble and would not follow Mrs. Fortune's directions. At the end of the day, Mrs. Fortune sent a note home with Johnny telling his mama that he had been in trouble most of the day. The following morning Mrs. Fortune was called to the office on the intercom and that she had a telephone call. Picking up the phone, she heard Johnny's mama say, "I just don't know what I am going to do with Johnny? Some days I feel like killing myself!" Mrs. Fortune slapped her hand over her mouth and said. "I wish you would!" Mrs. Fortune then turned to the secretary and said, "She hung up on me.," as she returned to her room. About thirty minutes later, she was once again called to the office and it was the Superintendent of Schools. He said, "Why did you tell that mother to kill herself?" Mrs. Fortune explained to the Superintendent that it was just a phrase she used and she would immediately call the mama and explain.

Dr. J. Terry Hall

Chapter 16

My grandson, Anthony is a pretty smart cookie. When he was only three he was putting things together by association.

There is a store on Dogwood Road near my son, Ben's house. The store had been there for years and the owners were doing some major reconstruction. As they were required by law, the owners had a portable outhouse placed in the lot for the workers to use. Ben had always called the business, "The Store." One day I was taking Anthony over to my house, when he looked out the window, and seeing the store and the outhouse in the lot, he yelled out, "Pee Store!" If that wasn't using association, I don't know what it was.

Dr. J. Terry Hall

In 1986, I was teaching at Vance Elementary School in Asheville, North Carolina. Roy Harwood, was serving as principal. Mr. Harwood was not only a great principal; he was a master woodcarver.

We were scheduled to move into a new school building the following year and Mr. Harwood decided to create a giant wood carving of Zeb Vance's Birthplace. Zeb Vance was Governor of North Carolina during the Civil War and was born near Asheville where his birthplace now stands.

Mr. Harwood, asked all his teachers to help him create the woodcarving. Billy Lewis and I volunteered. We worked after school and during summer vacation. After several months, the woodcarving was completed and was hung with pride just inside the front door of the new school building. Roy Harwood, Billy Lewis, and myself burned our names into the wood at the bottom of the work.

A few months passed and a visitor came into the school for the first time and commented on how beautiful the finished work looked. She noticed the names at the bottom of the creation and said, "Oh, I see you are also a woodcarver." To which I replied, "Oh No, Roy Harwood is the woodcarver, I am only a wood picker."

Dr. J. Terry Hall

Back in the day, I volunteered with the Asheville Area Rescue Squad. I had received my Emergency Medical Technician (EMT) training and was on call anytime I was not teaching, day or night.

One Saturday afternoon my tones sounded and I was informed that an attempted suicide was taking place just down the road from where I lived. I jumped into my red Ford pickup truck, turned on my red light and responded to the scene. I arrived just as an Asheville Police Officer was pulling into the drive. We did not know what method the victim had used, whether it had been an overdose, a gun, or what. The officer instructed me to stay behind him as he knocked loudly on the door with his gun in hand.

A woman came to the door and immediately slammed it shut. The officer re-opened the door and with gun drawn slipped into the kitchen calling out to the victim. I was following close behind the officer and shaking like a leaf on a windy day. Was she standing around the corner with a shotgun waiting to blow our heads off as we rounded the corner or not? That was the question running through my mind.

We heard a door slam shut down the hall as we made the turn into the hallway. Walking down the hallway, the officer and I stood on each side of the bedroom door as he knocked loudly while calling out to the woman to open the door. No sound came from the bedroom. This lasted for at least five minutes, which seemed like an hour to me. Just then, the minister from the local church came around the corner, walked up to the door, and shouted. "Lucy! If you are going to kill yourself go ahead and do it. I'm getting sick and tired of coming up here every time you want some attention. The woman slowly opened the door and the minister entered. I shook my head and I let out a sigh of relief. My thanks go to the police for what they have to endure on a daily basis.

Dr. J. Terry Hall

When our son was a baby and still in his crib, my wife, Patricia went into his room to check on him. Immediately, she screamed, "Snake, Snake!" as she ran backwards across the room. Ben, started to cry as I rushed into the room. By this time, Patricia had identified the problem.

It seemed that Ben had pulled off his diaper and shoo-shooed in the bed. What she thought was a snake, was a turd.

Dr. J. Terry Hall.

When I was around three-years-old, my mother asked me to go into her bedroom and bring her a bra. Being a good son, I went in and looked all over the bed. I could see no bra anywhere. I came back to her and said, "I couldn't find no bra, just this titty holder.

Dr. Terry Hall

During WWII, Patricia's daddy, Ben Cochran, served as an Army Medic aboard a transport ship. Throughout the war, he made three trips around the world. His duty was to take care of the Army personnel aboard the transport ship.

On this one occasion, they shipped out of San Diego bound for the war zone. In a short time, one of the Army personnel came to Ben and asked where the life preservers were stored. Ben thought it was odd that this routine precaution had not taken place, sobeing the Superior Officer over the Army personnel he approached the Captain and said, "Some of the men are wondering where the life perseveres are stored."

The Captain walked over to the intercom and made this announcement. "It has been brought to my attention that some of you are wondering where the life preservers are stored. Just for your information, we are carrying ten tons of TNT. If we are hit, you will not need a life persevere, you will need a damn parachute, because you will be going up, not down." Such comforting words were never spoken.

Dr. J. Terry Hall

My son Ben is a great father as he is always teaching his children how to be respectful adults. Even more important, he is a good example before them. One of the things he teaches the children is to pick up things after they get through playing. He told them, "If you see any trash on the floor, please pick it up and put it in the trash.

Well, one day Ben had just cashed a check for one hundred dollars and the bank had given him a one hundred dollar bill. Later in the day, he needed to go to the store and reached into his pocket. There was no large bill. He searched all over the house and in his car with no success. Finally, he pulled a one dollar bill out of his pocket and asked the children, "Have you seen anything like this?" Holding up the one dollar bill?" Robby said, "Yes daddy, I put it in the trash can just like you told us to."

Ben rushed to the trash can as he heard a roaring sound. He stopped in his tracks, looked across the yard and saw the trash truck moving down the road with his one hundred dollar bill. What could he do? Robby had done just what his daddy had told him, put the trash in the trash can.

Dr. J. Terry Hall

I attended a small country church as a child and the men who made sure everything that was taught was according to the Bible, were called Elders. There were three Elders serving at the church at that time. One of the Elders was as country as cornbread.

We had a very old man in the church by the name of Jack Carter. Brother Carter was very ill for a very long time and finally he died in his sleep. One of the Elders by the name of John Jones was directed to announce Brother Carter's death. After his other announcements, he said, "Also, Brother Carter finally passed out!" Everyone in the audience had to place their hand over their mouths to keep from laughing.

Dr. J. Terry Hall

I enjoyed going to college at Lindsey Wilson College. I was only eighteen years old and had never been this far from home alone. Although, I was only forty-five miles from home, I felt I was on my own.

In addition to studying, playing around and dating,(not necessarily in that order,) I had a lot of fun and made some lifetime friends. The story I am about to tell is one where I really crossed the line.

I was assigned a room on the third floor of the old dorm. There was a fire escape just outside my room which I shared with three more boys. It was a small room with four bunk beds and one table.

One day, someone came up with what seemed like a good plan at the time. Since there was a driveway just below the fire escape, we would take water balloons and drop them onto cars as they came onto campus. We did this and laughed and laughed. Then, I crossed the line. I said, "If we really want to have some fun, let's fill up the large trash can with water and dump it onto the next car to come onto campus." I then directed the operation with all my knowledge.

I assigned two big strong boys to hold the trash can and I would be the look-out. When I saw a car entering the campus, I would give them the signal and they would dump the big trash can of water over the edge of the window. Will that be fun, or what?

Well, I saw a brand new red convertible with the top down come in as I said, "Now!" The water was a direct hit and the convertible was flooded. The upper classman looked up, jumped out of his car and ran toward the dorm.

In less than a minute, we could hear him banging on dorm doors coming down the hallway. He was cussing at the top of his voice as he demanded to know who did such a thing. When we opened our door, all of us were sitting around the table studying for our test. We were shocked that anyone would stoop that low to do such an action.

Dr. J. Terry Hall

Another story I will share was about a boy that would party most of the night and then go to sleep during first period English class.

Like normal, he fell fast to sleep and at the end of the class, the teacher motioned to the students to slip quietly out of the class and she stepped to the door and held a finger up to her lips for them to be quiet as they entered.

About half way through the second period, the boy woke to find himself in another class and all his class was gone. He grabbed his books and ran out the door as everyone laughed, especially the teacher.

Dr. J. Terry Hall

One of my friends has two daughters and both of them are very smart. When the youngest daughter started kindergarten, my friend was taking her to school when she said from the back seat, "Pap-paw, give me some math problems to do. He said, "What is two plus two?" She immediately said, "Four, give me a hard one." He said, "What is five plus two? He could see her in the mirror as she counted on her fingers. She said, "Give me a really really hard one." He said, "What is eight plus eight?" As he watched her in the mirror, she counted all her fingers and then asked, "Pap-Paw, can I take off of my hoes?"

Dr. J. Terry Hall

---

worked for several years with the Haunted House around Halloween. I always dress as Michael Myers and have a butcher knife in my hand to scare people as they come through. I love playing Michael Myers and seeing everybody scream, especially teenaged girls when they come by my area. I have several tattoos on my legs and arms and one of them is Michael Myers

A few years ago I was in full costume over in Hendersonville, North Carolina when a group of teenaged girls passed by. I went into my act and the girls all screamed.

On this one occasion, I had taken my first child, Dakota along with me to the Haunted House. Dakota was sitting on one of my friend's knees when the teenage girls started screaming. Dakota climbed down off my friend's knee, walked over to one of the girls and asked, "Why are you afraid? That is just my daddy."

I thought, well he just blew my role as Michael Myers, when one of the girls asked "What is his name?" Dakota calmly said, "Michael Myers." All girls started screaming as I grabbed Dakota, threw him over my shoulder and ran off down the hallway.

Ben F. Hall

My Grandfather moved from Robeson County, N.C. To Rocky Mount, N.C. looking for a job with the railroads, as he was a younger son and could not inherit the family farm. Upon arrival, he learned there had been a plantation with the name of "Bullock." as the owners. This was very embarrassing to him as he did not want to be associated with the Bullock name. So, when filling out job and government forms, he changed the spelling of the family name to Bulluck." Our family never knew this until two generations later.

Beth Bulluck Carter

Printed in the United States
By Bookmasters